# Living in My Skin, Even if it's Purple

Debbie Fox

Copyright © 2011 by Debbie Fox


ISBN 978-0-7414-6748-5  Paperback
ISBN 978-0-7414-9519-8  eBook


Printed in the United States of America


Published December 2011

INFINITY PUBLISHING
1094 New DeHaven Street, Suite 100
West Conshohocken, PA 19428-2713
Toll-free (877) BUY BOOK
Local Phone (610) 941-9999
Fax (610) 941-9959
Info@buybooksontheweb.com
www.buybooksontheweb.com

# Acknowledgments

God designed me to be different. At times I thought it highly unfair, but I learned to accept myself and give him thanks, realizing that this was his plan for me. He opened my mind to understanding and provided me with the ability to write my story.

I thank my parents for believing in all my dreams. They instilled in me a resilience to overcome my difference and to embrace life with courage. I am forever grateful for their love and support.

For my former colleagues in Working Writers Critique Group, your suggestions have been invaluable. When I was tangled in fragments and wordiness, you steered me back on course. You have been beacons in my life.

I thank Susan Corner, teacher at College of the Canyons in Valencia, California, who was responsible for my first essay publication. You gave me hope of further publishing successes. And Dr. Floyd Moos, Dean of Fine & Performing Arts at College of the Canyons, my creative nonfiction writing instructor, thank you for helping me see the subtleties of the world around me, for reminding me to find a spark that ignites a torrent of memories so I might transform blank pages into a respectable piece of writing.

Finally, I thank all my dear friends who patiently listened to me bemoan my failures and gloriously celebrated with me every triumph. They pushed me to be more than I was and never lost faith in me. Thanks to my fellow writers in the St. Louis Writers Guild for support and friendship.

To the readers, I hope that *Living in My Skin* will resonate with anyone who has felt different, inspire self-acceptance, and serve as a stimulus to others to move beyond our differences.

# Disclaimer

Memories dim with the passage of time; however, some memories remain acutely clear, forever replayed. This book is written from my perspective, from *my* memories. The names have been changed to insure privacy, but the real people behind the pseudonyms were very special to me because they helped make this memoir. I highly respected every doctor and nurse who cared for me. In no way did I intend to disparage anyone depicted in this book.

# Dedication

For my family: Don, Mae, Roger, and Diane.
And for Kobe, my Coton de Tulear dog,
who can't read but has been a very patient companion.

# Table of Contents

**California Dreams**

# Living in My Skin, Even if it's Purple

*And God said, Let us make man in our image, after our likeness . . .*

*Gen.1:26*

## Grade School Survival

### CHAPTER ONE—AM I DIFFERENT?

It wasn't a secret; in fact, it was so obvious that people often gasped, yet my parents never talked with me about it. For them it was easier to ignore the problem and pretend normality. Where they saw only perfection in their firstborn child, others saw tragedy. In later years, I asked my parents all my plaguing questions, but everything was "fine," no difficulties remembered. Without a dangerous excavation, I could not unearth my parents' disappointment they hastily buried in 1951. Their reticence during my childhood made me fearful of probing too deeply, so I pretended all was "fine" and kept quiet. In my silence, my secrets remained buried.

\*     \*     \*

1

I first realized I was different when I was six years old. I lived with my parents and brother in a two-bedroom frame house at the end of a short gravel road. The two school-age girls across the street were my only playmates except for my baby brother, a scrawny three-year-old who shared my bedroom. Although I was eager to attend school, my neighborhood in Belleville, a small southern Illinois town, did not have a kindergarten. While waiting to start first grade, I unknowingly enjoyed my last days of innocence.

I loved to run in our huge yard, dodge puny fruit trees, and sprint past the forsythia bushes. Mom claimed I toddled across the street at nine months and, ever since, she's had a hard time restraining me. One day, I charged up our gravel driveway as if rabid dogs chased me. Suddenly, I stumbled over my feet and fell. I slid on my belly, my outstretched arms raking along the rocks. When I stopped in a puff of dust, blood leaked from my right arm faster than I could comprehend my injury. I burst into tears and dashed toward the house, trying to outrun my terror.

Mom, frightened by my howls, wrapped my lacerated arm, but the bleeding continued . . . and continued . . . before it trickled to a stop a half hour later. Mom whispered on the phone to Grandma, "I couldn't stop the bleeding."

After my bleeding incident, Mom warned me not to hurt my right arm. I didn't understand what she meant. Was it okay to hurt my left arm? She also wouldn't let the doctor give me a shot in my right arm, only the left one. But I didn't understand. Then I noticed my arms were different— different colors. My brother had two white arms, so did Mom and Dad, so did everyone I knew. Although puzzled by my discovery, I didn't ask Mom to explain my difference. I kept my questions to myself.

However, curiosity over my arm dilemma compelled me to examine photographs of myself. Displayed in the living room, a professionally altered black-and-white studio portrait hid what I would have to live with daily and showed me what I should have looked like. I found evidence of the real me in snapshots, the ones Mom secured in her photo album with small, black adhesive triangles. In one picture, taken when I was about a year old, I perched on a kitchen counter top, my head turned slightly over the strap of my frilly sun suit. Although the black-and-white picture softened the reality, the blotches on my right arm, back, chest, and neck appeared like dark cloud formations on an unspoiled canvas.

I was born with a birthmark.

Doctors called my birthmark a port wine stain, like the color of a rich port wine. While some colored areas ranged in hue from a pale rosé to a dark zinfandel, other areas were as dark as grape juice; moreover, the colored patches felt warmer compared to my white skin and turned shades darker whenever I was cold. The birthmark's texture, as smooth as my white skin, didn't curtail the shock. In the fifties, doctors didn't know much about birthmarks but discouraged skin grafts to hide the purple color because the grafts were as unsightly as the purple coloring. My parents agreed with the doctors. I would live with the irregular color splashes. By the time I was six, my parents had learned to ignore my difference and treated me as if I were the same as any other kid.

Never realizing I was truly different, I started first grade. Miss Trainer, the first grade teacher, exuded kindness, vitality, and patience as she awakened our minds. I liked her from the beginning. Liking all my classmates was another matter.

3

"What's that red stuff on your arm?" a freckle-faced girl named Lois asked.

"Nothing," I mumbled, instantly aware that I should know the answer but didn't. A strange feeling of shame came over me as if Mom had just caught me making ugly faces at my brother. Unable to explain, I sank lower in my desk.

"Did you paint your arm?" a chubby boy in the back row asked.

I buried my nose in my wide-lined pad of paper, fiddled with my new plump pencil, and tried to look busy, but their questions lingered in my mind. "What was that red stuff on my arm?" I wondered, and stole a peek at the offensive arm. Mom once told me it was my birthmark as if saying, "Yes, that's your ear." I didn't understand what a birthmark was. Would it go away? Would it get bigger? Was it catching? Since neither Mom nor Dad talked with me about my birthmark, I concluded that the subject, like bad words, shouldn't be mentioned, so I locked away my questions.

Despite my confusion, I tried to be a good student, tried to be as quiet and unobtrusive as possible, and tried not to cry like my baby brother when classmates teased me. Lois, the freckle-faced, smart-mouthed girl in my class, tormented me the most. I hated her.

Tall for a first grader, Lois displayed the athletic ability of a fifth grader. Whether swinging effortlessly on the trapeze bar or climbing like a squirrel on the jungle gym, she hurled barbs in my direction. "Debbie's got a red arm. Debbie's got a red arm," her singsong voice rang over the playground.

I wanted to bury her head in the sand beneath the high jump standard. I wanted to yell, "Shut up!" I wanted to run and hide; instead, I pretended not to hear words meant to inflict the first of many scars on my soul. Suffering shame was a burden, a tough and solitary assignment for a six-year-old.

The day Lois fell off the monkey bars and broke her arm was the best day of first grade. With Lois sporting a pasty white cast, the wisecracking boys laughed at her misfortune. Sidelined from the playground equipment, Lois sulked and lost some of her nastiness, but she never passed up an opportunity to needle me.

While I became aware of my difference, I quietly fell in love with Jeff, who sat next to me in class. He stole my heart because he never teased me. Although Jeff didn't know I considered him my boyfriend, I told my parents he was to satisfy their concerns about my adjustment to school. To this day, Mom remembers my first grade infatuation with Jeff. I remember an awakening awareness, seeing myself for the first time as others saw me, seeing my difference. My awareness baffled me. I didn't understand why Lois was cruel while Jeff was nice, so I shuttered my confusion inside, away from the light of reason.

In my baby book, my mother describes me at birth as "adorable, intelligent, beautiful, and a complete joy." She writes that I had "dark curly hair, blue eyes, and a beautiful face" and "all the nurses thought [I] was the prettiest baby they had ever seen." Neither Mom nor Dad mentioned my birthmark. Neither saw my difference.

Reading Mom's entry reminded me of the day my brother accidentally broke one of two plaster casts of my handprints. Before I could pound the living daylights out of him, Mom interceded with a promise to fix the plaque.

5

"It's not the same," I sobbed upon seeing Mom's repair job. "It's not perfect."

Mom surveyed the two casts side-by-side and said, "I hardly notice the difference."

*    *    *

# CHAPTER TWO—STOP PICKING ON ME!

Whenever her grandchildren were within earshot of an inappropriate topic of conversation, Grandma often muttered, "Little feet have big ears." Whether cutting potatoes at the kitchen table or shucking corn on the back porch, the women in my family loved to talk, or more aptly put—gossip. They scrutinized marriages and child rearing, predicted the sex of unborn babies, dickered over the best method of cleaning windows, and argued about who sold the freshest eggs. Like hot gravy, their German blood boiled during the more lively coffee klatches. An "Ach du liebe Zeit" or "Gott im Himmel" bubbled to the surface when their passion threatened to overflow the pot. While not exactly eavesdropping on the heated clan, I picked up an education. Some information I heard scared me more than the black-and-white monster movies Mom didn't know my brother and I watched. But some lessons proved vital to my elementary school survival.

Before I started second grade, my family moved across town to a new house Dad and his two brothers built. I don't think the house was ready for us. Located on an afterthought gravel road, the red-brick, ranch house bordered a cornfield and weedy land owned by the family. Beyond one open field, the family business, a concrete construction company, sat on the main highway that led to the subdivision. Dad, a civil engineer, designed our home (with many recommendations from Mom) and supervised its construction. Although the house was unfinished, my parents moved us in. My young eyes never noticed the plywood floors, unpainted walls, empty rooms, and unadorned windows because my very own bedroom claimed my attention. I no longer had to share a room or a set of bunk beds with my little brother Roger; consequently, I embraced my independence and treasured my privacy.

While Mom carved personality into our new house, I began second grade like an uninvited guest—the school year had already started. To show me the ropes, I latched on to Barbara, the daughter of family friends.

My first day of school, I boarded the bus and took a seat next to Barbara and her friend Lucy. After a three-mile trip, the school bus shuddered to a halt in the shadow of an intimidating brick building that seemed taller than two stories. Merging with the lunch-box-toting pack, I followed Barbara up a steep driveway that led to a blacktop playground surrounded by grassy baseball fields.

"We can't go inside until the bell rings," Barbara quietly instructed.

Barbara and Lucy, both as unassuming as clouds, hugged the side of the building next to the door. While I waited to enter, I watched my fellow students and wondered how I would fit in. The students, who had spent the last two years together, had formed cliques that a newcomer would not be able to infiltrate. When the fateful bell sounded, I filed inside with my new best friends, afraid of what I might find.

Miss Duckworth, the second grade teacher, frowned as she assigned me a desk. She was about as welcoming as a prison warden. With a forced smile, I headed for my seat, conscious that every eye in the room followed me, staring at my red arm. I slipped into my seat and pretended not to notice my classmates' inspection.

With a sigh, Miss Duckworth rose from behind her massive desk and clomped across the wooden floor in her lace-up grandma shoes. She delivered the lesson, shouting like the minister on Sunday mornings. I understood the class work, yet fearful of sounding too smart or too stupid, I hesitated to volunteer. When the bell announced recess, I almost flew out the door.

After recess, Miss Duckworth lost steam and droned on until she dismissed the class for lunch. Later, a game of kickball injected life into the middle of a long afternoon. By three-thirty, my homework assignments packed up, I fled with my classmates to the bus for home.

Wearing a big smile, Mom greeted me at the front door, "How was school?"

"Fine," I answered, not wanting to destroy her happiness.

"Did you make any new friends?"

"Just a couple."

"Did you like your teacher?"

"She's okay." I couldn't tell her Miss Duckworth was an old battle-ax and yelled a lot. I didn't want to go back to school where the teacher frightened me and my classmates studied me like a new subject, but I did.

My second grade class at Lincoln School contained twice as many girls as boys. Half the girls outweighed all the boys and towered inches above their flattops. I fell into the remaining half of the girls—short and skinny with legs like bicycle spokes. My half of the group, more reserved than the other half, bore the brunt of childhood brutality. With difficulty, I digested the teasing served up daily as the blue-plate special of second grade. The big girls, who would develop breasts in the fourth grade and start their periods the following year, taunted us smaller girls.

"Don't go outside today," big Brenda warned me. "The wind might blow you away."

"When ya gonna put some meat on those bones?" Terri asked me, and I couldn't help but notice the rolls of flesh hiding her bones.

One of my classmates suffered more teasing than the rest of us. Not only was Minnie's name a strike against her, but she was also short and skinny, nearsighted and cockeyed. She had spells where she stared vacantly at the ceiling or sky, not speaking or moving for a minute. "Four eyes," one teaser jeered. "Wait, Minnie's getting an idea," another said and laughed at Minnie in her trance-like state. When Minnie's seizure ended, she continued her previous activity and ignored the taunts.

Another classmate, a boy named Barry, lugged around a briefcase like an F.B.I. agent. Although Barry seemed calm and quiet, suddenly, in the middle of one of Miss Duckworth's lectures, he would vomit his breakfast or lunch.

Whenever Barry would barf, Miss Duckworth would quickly grab her long stick with its crooked nail at the end, rattle the nail into the keyhole at the top of the twenty-foot window, and yank open the window to air the room. The janitor, with his bucket of odor-absorbing wood shavings, would regularly visit our classroom to mop up the messes, but the smell would stick to Barry all week. Friendless and alone with his secretive briefcase, Barry accepted his teasing as easily as he accepted his vomiting.

As another oddity in the second grade class, I suffered from teasing, too, mostly from a gang of rowdy boys.

"Hey kid, where'd ya get that red stuff on your arm?" one brute yelled.

"Betcha she burned herself playing with matches," another boy said.

"Just ignore them," my new friend Barbara whispered.

"Are you an Indian?" one of the boys asked. "How," he said as he raised his arm like Tonto and laughed.

The gang took turns getting in their licks, perhaps hoping I would start crying like Mary in my class, who sniffled whenever she didn't get her way. I took Barbara's advice, turned my back on the boys, and walked away.

After weeks of harassment, I decided I didn't want the teasing to continue. I didn't want to be like Minnie, ignoring the ugliness, or like Barry who didn't have any friends. I had to do something to stop the torment. I wanted to tell the teacher, but she only cared that I address her by Miss, not Mrs. Duckworth, and goose bumps raised on my arms whenever I thought to approach her. I also never told Mom about the teasing.

One day while visiting Grandma, I heard her yell from the porch, "You boys, I see you climbing on my fence. Get down from there. Right now! Before I tell your momma. And don't you be fixin' to shinny up that tree." Grandma shook her finger at the boys, and they obeyed. Despite Grandma's small size and crooked back, she loomed large enough to scare off the boys. She wasn't afraid of them and didn't tolerate any nonsense. That day, I decided to be more like Grandma. I wouldn't let the rowdy boys tease me any longer. I'd stand up for what was proper.

When I returned to school, one of the boys said, "We're not playing Indians today, so take your red skin home."

I drew in a breath and fired. "So what if I have red skin. You're nothing but a dirty, filthy ragamuffin, and nobody likes you."

The gang of boys laughed at my insult, but my tormentor scowled and tried again. "You're as red as the devil," he said with a sneer, confident his barb would make me run.

I threw one hand on my hip, poised for a counterattack. "You are a devil," I shot back. "You probably had a hard time hiding your tail in your tight britches this morning."

The gang roared with laughter and slapped backs until my tormentor pivoted and marched off in defeat. My meek girlfriends stared at me as if I were a stranger. I smiled wide enough for everyone to notice and sashayed toward the school door. Even Miss Duckworth couldn't wipe the happiness off my face.

\*       \*       \*

# CHAPTER THREE—GUILT, PRAYERS, AND CONFUSION

During the next three years, my sassiness sustained me while shame eroded my soul. In Sunday school, I learned the Golden Rule, "Do to others as you would have them do to you." Was I any better than my school tormentors? Although my smart comebacks stemmed some of the teasing, I felt guilty and sinful. Unable to decide on a more appropriate method of dealing with the taunts, I prayed for answers and hoped I wouldn't go to Hell.

Meanwhile, Mom, still oblivious to my difference, sensed I needed socialization and enrolled me in a baton class. Sporting bruises and chipped fingernails from twirling exercises, I practiced coordination and discipline. With my fellow twirlers busy learning flat flams and figure eights, they didn't have time to comment on my strange appearance.

In the beginner baton class, I endlessly rehearsed a routine. I learned to march in time to music and to count silently in my head so each executed movement coincided with my classmates'. While "The Thunderer" blared from the record player, I marched in place, performed basic twirls, and attempted grace and poise. "Smile," my teacher reminded me.

When the day of my first baton recital arrived, Mom fussed over me as if I had an audition with a talent scout. After hours in prickly curlers, my hair uncoiled with a bounce . . . until Mom formed a sausage-roll curl that encircled my head below my ears and cemented it in place with hairspray. My butterscotch outfit revealed more skin than the clothes I normally wore, but it was my day to be a performer.

"Let me put some makeup on you," Mom offered.

"Okay." I jumped at the opportunity to wear the lipstick, eye shadow, and mascara like Mom wore on special occasions. Through my nine-year-old eyes, I watched in the mirror while Mom brushed color on my face. She frowned now and then as she perfected her portrait. When she was done, she grabbed several little white sponges and opened a jar I had never seen.

"What's that?" I asked.

She opened the jar. "Something to cover your birthmark."

"Oh." I was surprised to hear her mention my birthmark.

Mom dug into the jar with one of the little white sponges and smeared a glob of the thick, flesh-colored cream on my neck and right arm. She repeatedly dipped the white sponges into the jar, then smoothed the cream over my red and purple splotches. The makeup diminished the dark color of my port wine stain but didn't match the color of my normal arm. I guessed Mom thought it looked better than a red and purple arm. When she finished, I pranced in front of the mirror, undecided about my new look.

As I stood in the wings with my classmates, waiting to take the stage, I mentally rehearsed my routine and prayed I wouldn't drop my baton. No one commented on my altered appearance. My baton performance was as near to perfection as the makeup that hid my birthmark, and both must have made my mom proud because she snapped a lot of pictures.

After that first baton recital, Mom refrained from smearing makeup on me to cover my birthmark. Maybe she thought it was too much trouble. Although I hadn't liked how my arm felt with the makeup—all gooey and stiff—I had never complained to Mom. I ignored my redness and convinced myself that my baton twirling would compensate for my appearance.

When my baton teacher formed the troupe into a drill team, I marched my vanity down every main street of every town in the area. Although the sleeveless, turquoise outfit didn't hide my red arm, my teacher had the good sense to position me on the left side of the marching formation, where my right arm did not draw immediate attention. Along the parade route, all eyes couldn't help but notice the drill team's satin outfits, trimmed with white fringe and sequins, flashing as brightly as the batons. The short skirts flared and the white cowgirl hats stayed securely in place during the team's synchronized spins, kicks, and bends. Completing the uniform with turquoise snap-on cuffs and buffed white cowgirl boots, the team presented a sharp, crisp performance that drew loud applause from the crowd.

Similarly dressed, Carolyn, my teacher, strutted yards in front of the team, and she really put on a show. She heaved her baton thirty feet in the air and while the baton turned circles, Carolyn spun around and around like an ice skater until the baton dropped right into her waiting hand. With a wide smile and electric energy, her baton a flashing blur, Carolyn moved with grace and authority. I wanted to be just like her.

I felt proud when I marched with the team. I liked the spectators' smiles and applause. Occasionally, an observer in the crowd pointed at my red arm and exchanged words with the person standing next to them. I knew they were discussing my redness, but I didn't care. I was the performer, not the one standing on the sidelines. My glistening outfit and the silver shaft of my baton outshined my red arm. As a performer, absorbed in the routine, I forgot my difference and difficulties. Basking in the adoration of the crowd, I forgot my shame.

School days dragged along, and my sassiness (and guilt) continued. As my tormentors grew older, they became more sophisticated in their methods to wound me.

During recess, two girls from my class cornered me. One girl spoke out, "My momma said a birthmark is the sign of the devil. You must be a devil."

I scowled at her. "I am not."

"Are you sure you don't have horns under your hair?" She wrinkled her nose while she stared into my hair.

I pointed my finger at her. "You're the devil."

"My mother said your mom was frightened by something horrible when she carried you inside her . . . before you were born," the other girl chimed in.

With my finger, I made circles in the air next to my ear. "You're both crazy."

The second girl continued her attack. "Your mom probably saw somebody's arm cut off or something worse. That's why you have a red arm."

"That's not true," I said with a shake of my head. "What did your mom see that made you so ugly?"

She lifted up her chin and cocked her head to one side. "I'm not ugly."

"You are too." I stuck out my tongue, packed up my guilt, and walked away. "Sticks and stones may break my bones, but words can never hurt me," I repeated to myself, but the girls' comments cut deep and haunted me. What if they were right? Maybe Mom had seen something awful. I remembered Uncle Charlie who had lost half a leg in a motorcycle accident. Was Mom carrying me then? Did she see his mangled leg? Did the devil mark me?

I prayed harder at Sunday school, hoping God would erase the mark I began believing the devil had made. At night, I smothered my sobs in my pillow so Mom and Dad wouldn't hear me. Wanting to look like the other kids, I prayed to Jesus for a white right arm, but in the morning, my arm gleamed like a ripe plum. My prayers went unanswered.

I wondered what compelled Mom to apply makeup to my arm before my recital. I didn't know Mom even noticed my birthmark; she never talked about it or asked me how I felt about it. Was she trying to cover up the devil's mark? I

17

didn't know what to think. Broaching the subject with Mom seemed taboo, so questions tumbled in my head, awaiting maturity for answers.

"Okay, boys, you may be excused," my fifth grade teacher announced one morning. The boys fled the stern gaze of Mrs. Biehl, and the girls looked knowingly at each other and tried not to giggle. "Settle down," Mrs. Biehl rasped, tapping her hooked-tip pointer on her desk, then used it to lower the white projection screen. "Someone, please draw the shades so we can get started."

The film, produced by Modess (rhymes with "oh yes"), flickered to life on the screen, instructing us girls on the facts of life—or at least menstruation. Mrs. Biehl hid in the back of the room, too old to be concerned with the changes occurring in young girls' bodies. The brief film left more questions in my mind than it answered, but Mrs. Biehl made it clear we should ask our mothers or the school nurse anything we didn't understand. She concluded our sex education class by handing us a booklet and dismissing us for recess.

"That's why Brenda and Phyllis carry those brown paper grocery bags once a month," Sarah, my new best friend, whispered to me on the way out. Sarah recently enrolled at my school when her dad was transferred to nearby Scott Field Air Force Base. Well-traveled and smart, Sarah skipped third grade. Like a fan club member, I gravitated to her, eager to hear stories of her past schools, neighborhoods, and friends. As we became closer, Barbara and Lucy's friendship wilted from my life.

"What's in their grocery bags?" I asked Sarah.

"Modess." She pronounced the word correctly.

I stopped walking. "You mean they already got their periods?"

Sarah nodded, stopping beside me. "Yes, Terri has started, too, I think." She lisped through her retainer.

"You are so smart, Sarah. I never guessed what was in the bags."

With a laugh, she shook her black, poker-straight pageboy. "Even the boys figured it out."

We exited the building and ambled onto the playground. "I can't believe I'm that stupid." I slapped my forehead. "Mom gave me 'the talk' a couple months ago, but she said 'it' might not happen for a couple of years."

"Well, not for them," she said.

"Have you . . .?" I whispered.

"No. They're just more developed than we are."

We both glanced at our chests and grinned.

Sarah brushed a lock of hair from her face. "You know, the boys had their talk today while we had ours."

"They learned about periods?"

"I don't know, but they sure are looking at us differently." Sarah rolled her coal black eyes toward a group of boys huddled nearby.

"It's too creepy to think about what they know." I turned my back on the group, feeling like an exhibit at the zoo, but not because of my port wine stain.

Now I had something else to worry about besides my birthmark and the Golden Rule—boys.

*     *     *

# CHAPTER FOUR—THE OUTSIDER

"Mom please, please may I go?" I squirmed in the front seat of the car. Mom ignored me and steered the '59 Ford toward home after my baton lesson. "You know Bev's parents." I switched the radio station to KXOK. Bobby Vee's voice crooned "Take Good Care of my Baby," and Mom shot me a look. "Jane and Darla were invited, too." I swayed to the music and watched Mom mull over my request.

Mom braked for a red light. "I understand Bev's invited boys to the party."

"Yeah, a few from her school—no one I know. It's gonna be a swell party. Please, please may I go?"

My whining worked because Mom agreed I could go to Bev's party. Bev lived across town and went to Countryside School. I met Bev, Jane, and Darla, all from different schools, in my baton class. I could hardly contain my excitement—my first real boy-girl party.

During the days before the party, I thought about how the new kids would react to my difference. I just wanted to fit in with the crowd, and I worried about what to wear. Ordinary school dresses wouldn't do, nor would fancy church clothes; consequently, I selected a pair of cotton slacks and a festive blouse. The Peter Pan collar of the short-sleeve blouse wouldn't cover my red neck or arm, but I couldn't wear a turtleneck sweater in the warm spring weather. Maybe the boys across town won't notice my difference.

Party day arrived and with it a case of nerves. Why did I talk Mom into letting me go to the party? What if the kids called me names and made fun of my birthmark? I tortured myself with a half dozen scenarios. I had been to boy-girl birthday parties but never to a boy-girl party that didn't require presents. I wondered what went on, certain it wasn't like any birthday party I had attended. "Come on," I told myself, "you're going to have a great time." I wasn't sure I believed myself.

"Debbie, are you about done primping?" Mom shouted from the kitchen.

"I'll be ready in a minute," I yelled. I sat at the vanity in my pink and white bedroom and stared into the tri-fold mirror. Beneath thick brows, blue eyes fringed with long lashes looked back at me and studied the ten-year-old girl. *I am pretty.* A small pug nose, salted with light freckles, centered my face. I practiced smiling, pleased to see two matching dimples form in my flawless cheeks. Straight teeth gleamed like pearls as I further perused my attributes. My blond hair that Mom described as a "dishwater" color curled in soft flips and hid small perfect ears. When my eyes focused lower in the reflection, I stopped smiling. Above and to the right of my collar billowed my birthmark. I swiveled to my right and lifted my chin-length hair, and I saw the top of the purple stain trail into my hairline. I quickly fluffed my hair back into place and wished it were a little longer.

"Debbie, we have to get going." Mom stood at my open bedroom door and startled me from my reverie.

I took one more glance in the mirror and bounced up.

Mom hugged me and planted a kiss on my forehead. "You look beautiful. Now get moving."

As Mom and I hurried through the family room on the way to the garage, Dad lowered his newspaper. "Have a good time."

My stomach fluttered with butterflies on the trip to Bev's house. Neither a dance recital nor a parade had stirred such a sensation. When we pulled up to the house, I could barely spit out a goodbye to Mom.

"Have fun, sweetheart," Mom said after the Baileys claimed possession of me.

"I will," I said with forced enthusiasm as Mom headed for the car.

"The kids are in the basement. I'll show you the way." Mr. Bailey escorted me inside and opened the basement door. Music drifted up the stairs. "Go on down and get yourself something to drink. The hot dogs and cake will be served later."

"Thank you for inviting me."

"You're welcome." Mr. Bailey chuckled. "Bev, Debbie's here," he shouted over the music.

23

Bev's moon-shaped face poked around the banister at the bottom of the steps. "Hi! Come meet the kids."

"Sure." I followed as if I had been summoned to the principal's office.

Crepe paper streamers and colorful balloons decorated the dimly lit basement. A table, laden with snacks, stood in one corner, soda iced in an aluminum washtub next to it. My eyes adjusted to the darkened room, and I noticed a few kids huddled around the record player.

Bev introduced me to the first guest. "This is Bobby."

Acting like a grown-up, I extended my right arm—my red and purple arm. When Bobby saw an arm thrust in front of him that looked as if it had soaked up grape juice, he momentarily froze. His eyes flitted from my alien appendage to my face, and his brows crunched together. I forced a nervous smile. "Nice to meet you."

Bobby grasped my hand as if it were a toad and he feared getting warts. He waved my arm up and down one time and then reeled in his hand. Glancing at his palm, he grinned. "Same here." He quickly retreated a step.

The other guests watched our introduction. Since Bobby survived his contact with my red palm, the others greeted me with less hesitancy. The tension inside me eased, and my forced smile turned genuine.

As more guests arrived, including Jane and Darla, conversation competed with the blaring music. Girls danced in a pack, throwing glances toward the boys, who were stuffing themselves with potato chips and covertly eyeing the girls. Periodically, Mrs. Bailey replenished the snacks before she delivered the promised hot dogs and cake. With a notice to call her should anyone need anything, she disappeared back up the stairs.

The food rapidly dwindled. Fueled by hot dogs, the dancers accelerated their motion, their moves poor imitations of "American Bandstand" dancers. Despite my dancing inexperience, I joined in the frenzy where my inhibitions vaporized among the vibrations. I flailed and swayed, jerked and gyrated, and forgot about being different. When the record player dropped the next plastic 45rpm on the turntable and "Blue Moon" seeped from the speaker, I found a chair and collapsed to collect my breath.

Suddenly, the lights dimmed.

"Let's play 'Spin the Bottle,'" someone suggested.

Cheers erupted around me. The guests moved aside chairs and tables and then sat in a circle on the carpeted area. I, too, dropped to the floor, eager to learn a new game. One of the girls laid an empty soda bottle in the middle of the circle and gave it a spin. "I'll go first."

I didn't understand the object of the game. The bottle stopped its spin; its mouth pointed to one of the boys in the circle. The girl, who had spun the bottle, leaned forward and kissed the boy on his cheek. I didn't know what to think. Bev smiled and clapped along with her school chums. Darla, sitting next to me, elbowed me in the ribs. I couldn't make out Jane's reaction in the poor light.

"My turn," said the next girl in the circle. She crawled to the bottle, gave it a spin, and scooted back to her place. When the bottle stopped, it pointed to a girl.

"Doesn't count. Spin again," Bev said.

The girl repeated the process as if it were a duty. This time the bottle pointed to a boy. The giggling girl hopped over to him and gave him a kiss. Everyone in the circle took a turn spinning the bottle and issuing a kiss. When it came my turn to spin, I pecked the designated boy like a striking snake. I popped back to my place in the circle, feeling as if I had done something wrong.

During the second round of spinning, the bottle pointed to me. The boy hesitated a moment, and I feared he would quit the game because he had to kiss me. He slowly approached me, then quickly planted a brotherly peck on my cheek. During the remainder of the round, the kids became more daring—kissing on the mouth. I took my cue from Jane and stuck to kissing on the cheek. By the luck of the spin, no boy had to mouth kiss me. I didn't know whether to be relieved or dismayed.

"Okay, final round." Bev pointed to the louver doors, which led, I supposed, to the laundry area. "You get two minutes back there . . . if you want."

A couple of willing participants ducked behind the doors. When they emerged, smiles lit their faces as if they knew a secret. I knew, without a doubt, I would not learn what went on behind the doors. The game ended, leaving me to wonder if a boy would ever kiss me . . . on the mouth. Would a boy want to escape with me to do whatever a boy does with a girl in private? I wasn't sure what went on, but I wanted to experience it. Inside I felt as normal as the other girls; outside I looked different. Would a boy see beyond my outside?

The lights came up and everyone looked embarrassed. Minutes later (Bev must have kept a close eye on the time) Mrs. Bailey, halfway down the stairs, announced, "Last call for cake. Parents will be here soon."

When Mom arrived, I mumbled my thanks and good-byes to Bev and her parents.

"How was the party?" Mom asked on the drive home.

"Fine," I said. Everything was always fine in my family.

\*      \*      \*

# CHAPTER FIVE—I HATE MY BODY!

Teetering on the perimeter of puberty, I finished my last year at Lincoln School as awkwardly as when I had started. Although I was preoccupied with my birthmark in my early school years, my scrawniness distressed me more as sixth grade graduation loomed ahead. My skinny arms, flat chest, and spindly legs refused to ripen into a womanly shape. Girls whose figures had rounded and attracted boys' attention laughed at my lack of development. The boys, who once teased me, now treated me with indifference. I still looked like a little girl.

The sex education pamphlet I had received in fifth grade described the changes that would occur in my body. I searched for a hint of maturity, unable to detect even a faint difference beneath my undershirt. Shaped like a clothespin, I wondered when I would see breasts and hips. I expected them to materialize overnight, but my development had stalled like a flooded Ford. Not one pimple poked its way through my creamy complexion. Not one hair sprouted where it never before had grown; however, the hair on my legs grew as if fertilized. And Mom wouldn't allow me to shave.

"Once you start shaving, you can never stop," Mom said. "And the hair only grows back faster and darker than before. Besides, you'll nick yourself and bleed and get scars."

I hated my body!

God gave me a birthmark, so why did he have to give me so much hair? From my dad, I inherited bushy eyebrows and hairy extremities. I prayed I wouldn't inherit his baldness, but Mom told me I had a "healthy head of hair." Although I rolled, brushed, teased, sprayed, and *smoothed* my locks into a stylish chin-length flip, the moment I stepped outside the house, my hair rippled like waves on a pond. I simply wished to look normal, but blaming fate or heredity would neither help my hair problems nor speed up my development.

Living in a neighborhood comprised solely of boys, I had no older girls with whom to compare myself, so I spied on the girls in my baton drill team while we dressed for parades. One thing I noticed was that no one had a half-purplish red chest like mine. My redness went clear down to my right nipple. I also noticed the older girls wore bras like my mom. In my undershirt, I tried to hide my puny, red-skinned body from the girls. I wished I didn't have a birthmark, but more importantly, I wanted to wear a bra and feel grown up.

During a family mid-winter vacation to Florida, my parents reconnected with old friends who had once lived in Belleville. Liz, Mom's friend since high school, and her husband had two girls, Valerie and Cindy, before they moved away to Miami. When Liz and Mom both became pregnant for the first time and went into labor at the same time, they shared a hospital room. I was born September first; Valerie was born September second. Since we had been playmates from an early age, Liz and Mom constantly compared our progress. That vacation was no exception.

One day, Liz and the girls came to visit us at our Miami Beach hotel where we had a spacious suite with a sitting room, a bedroom, and a large dressing area adjacent to the bathroom. While Liz and Mom chatted in the sitting room, Valerie and I experimented with makeup at the lighted vanity in the dressing area.

I couldn't help overhearing Mom ask Liz, "Has Valerie started to develop?"

Liz cackled. "Are you kidding? She's as much a tomboy as ever."

"Has she started yet?" Mom asked.

"Heavens no, but I think things are beginning to grow, if you know what I mean."

Valerie, who had been making faces in the mirror, turned to me when she heard her mother's words. Her brown eyes widened. I pressed my index finger to my lips to silence her forthcoming outburst.

The women continued their conversation, oblivious that Valerie and I were listening. "At first, I thought something was wrong with Valerie when she showed me," Liz said. "But I think she's getting breasts."

"I don't think Debbie's have begun to form."

31

"Maybe you should look at Valerie and tell me what you think," Liz suggested.

The two women suddenly appeared around the corner. "Val, pull up your shirt so Mae can look at your lump," Liz said as if she'd asked Valerie to show us her new ponytail ribbon.

"Moth-er!" Valerie groaned.

"Come on, show Mae your lump."

While I was a little curious, I felt Valerie's embarrassment. She silently raised her tee shirt, and Mom swooped in for a close inspection.

"Feel it, "Liz told Mom.

Tentative at first, Mom then touched Valerie's chest like a doctor performing an examination. "Yes, I feel something hard beneath her nipple. Are you sure this is normal?"

"Well, I can't remember myself at her age, but I think that's what's happening." Liz gave Valerie's chest a quick feel.

"Perhaps the doctor should check her," Mom said.

Valerie rolled her eyes at me, and I shook my head in disbelief.

"Let's see what you have under your shirt," Liz said, pointing to me.

I thought I would faint.

Mom waggled her finger at me. "Go on. Pull up your shirt, so we can check you."

Under the glare of the vanity lights, I yanked up my shirt, turned my head to the side, and sucked in a breath. The two mothers palpated my chest while I pictured a horse undergoing a similar inspection at an auction. I hoped Valerie's sister, my brother, and Dad wouldn't rush through the door at that moment.

"Yep, I can feel a hard nodule on the right side," Liz said.

"Me too," Mom concurred.

Wow, I guess I did notice the tiny bud, but I thought a muscle had developed from my baton twirling. *Gee, I must be growing up.* With the dignity of a lady, I refrained from whooping and hollering my happiness.

Liz smiled at Valerie and me. "Our girls will be women soon." She chuckled as she and Mom returned to the sofa to discuss their next topic.

Valerie and I stared at each other for a split second, and then we burst into giggles. I may have been born first, but Valerie's development exceeded mine. I wondered how fast my tiny bud would grow and when the second one would begin. By graduation day, a few months away, I figured I'd be wearing a bra. Unfortunately, I underestimated my calculation by a year.

After my Florida vacation, I returned to school a changed girl, elated by my budding development but devastated to learn I needed glasses. A couple weeks after my visit to the eye doctor, I received my new glasses. The doctor claimed the powder blue frames complimented my

# Teenage Trials

## CHAPTER SIX—HOW DO I FIT IN?

The first half of seventh grade, the year my straight A's earned me St. Louis Cardinals baseball tickets, was a disappointment. The breasts I didn't see at sixth grade graduation finally appeared but looked as flat as the plains of Illinois. Boys avoided me for whatever reason, and class schedules separated my girlfriends and me. Although I marched and twirled with adequate ability and excelled at swimming, my ineptitude for sports excluded me from the more popular school athletic crowd. The instruction I received in confirmation lessons molded my conscious to prevent me from hanging out with the "fast" crowd (not that they would consider throwing out their welcome mat for me). It was a year of expectation, a year of highs and lows, and a year of adjustment.

Four or five grade schools funneled into South Junior High School, an ancient brick building a couple blocks south of the town square. Two blacktop areas served as the baseball field and the exercise yard for physical education

37

classes. All the bricks, concrete, and blacktop smothered me. The only greenery in sight was the straggly bushes next to the entrance.

The first day of school, I located my homeroom in the lower level where its small windows provided a glimpse of the newspaper office across the street. The teacher, Miss Gold, a small woman with big hair, arranged the students alphabetically, placing me between a Smith and a Williams. None of my friends had been assigned to my homeroom, but I hoped to see them at lunch. I missed Sarah, her arm frantically waving like a referee when she knew the answer to the teacher's question. I missed Mary, even if she easily cried.

After homeroom, lines of students stood elbow to elbow at the banks of lockers in the hall outside the classroom. The empty slot in the corner matched my assigned number. I tried the combination and then yanked on the handle, but nothing happened. After verifying the combination, I tried again. The handle wouldn't budge. An exasperated sigh escaped my lips. I heard a chorus of banging metal from slamming locker doors. Students shuffled off. I fretted I'd be late for class. Sweat dampened my forehead as I bent over the dial and twisted it. "Please open," I prayed. Nothing. "What am I doing wrong?" I said to no one in particular.

"Ya need some help?" a voice behind me asked.

I turned around to face dreamy blue eyes and dimples. I remembered him from homeroom, but I couldn't speak.

"Let me try. I promise I won't break into your locker." The boy snatched the paper with the combination from my hand.

I moved my tongue around my sand-filled mouth and finally spit out, "That would be great."

In seconds, the boy whipped through the combination, raised the silver handle, and opened the door. "There ya go." He grinned with a crooked-tooth smile.

"Th . . . tha . . . thanks," I said.

"You probably didn't dial two times past the second number. Try it again," he said as he shut the door.

I slowly twisted the dial as he suggested. When I pulled on the handle, the door opened. "Yeah! Hey, thanks a lot."

"Well, I gotta get going."

"Me too. And thanks again." I watched him lope down the hall and turn the corner. *He didn't even tell me his name.* I thought as I rushed to my class.

Confusion predominated that first day of junior high school. Between classes, familiar faces passed me in halls that bulged with students, but the five-minute interval offered little time for socializing. By lunch, I felt like a mouse in a maze, hungry for my reward.

I zipped through the lunch line and spied Sarah and Mary approaching a table. As I caught up with them and we were about to take our seats, a boy at the next table said, "This table is for eighth graders."

"Oh, we didn't know." I looked around at the clusters of tables filled with students.

He nodded his head toward the other side of the room. "Over there."

The lights in the gym faded. "Listen, the music's starting," I said. From around me, girls descended to the gym floor in their stocking feet.

"Looks like it's time to twist and shout." Sarah tore off her shoes, tossed them aside, and leaped to the floor.

I took off my shoes and set them neatly on a bench and then hesitantly followed my friends, my stocking feet skating across the floor. The boys roosted high in the bleachers and watched us like eagles stalking prey. When the string of fast songs ended and I had worked up a sweat, Bobby Vinton's recorded voice punctuated the words to "Blue Velvet." Some of the boys dived into the throng of girls and selected partners for the slow dance. They swooped up girls until I stood alone among the couples, a spectacle for the boys who watched from their nests. Hoping no one would notice me, I shuffled back to my shoes and glimpsed dreamy blue eyes and dimples in the bleachers, laughing with his buddies. Tears stung my eyes, but I tried to hide my disappointment. As I watched the couples, I took comfort that dreamy blue eyes and dimples wasn't dancing with anyone. I still had hope.

Andy, dreamy blue eyes and dimples, was not only in my homeroom but also in my Saturday morning confirmation class. At school, I trailed him like a puppy and found any excuse just to be near him. In confirmation class, I beamed smiles in his direction whenever he glanced my way, but he rarely spoke to me. When he noticed my interest in him, he dodged me as if I were an incoming missile.

I forced myself to attend other school dances, hoping Andy or any boy would take pity on me and ask me to dance. One did.

Jimmy enjoyed dancing with many girls. He would wander the field of wallflowers and pluck one for a dance. Whenever Jimmy picked me and transplanted me in his arms for two or three minutes, I bloomed. My heart thudded as I placed my hand on the shoulder of his sweater, the wool scratchy beneath my fingers. His left hand, as warm as fresh baked bread, clutched my chilly red one, and with his right arm resting firmly against my back, he took the lead. I followed his two-step, inhaling his scent that smelled as if he had bathed in his dad's aftershave. I liked that Jimmy cared about us wallflowers. Although he was nice, I didn't see him as a boyfriend.

The independent Andy attracted me from the first day I saw him. I longed to drown in his pool-water eyes and feel his saving arms around me. I wanted to see him smile at me so I could watch his dimples deepen and treasure a glimpse of his crooked-tooth grin. Although I danced where Andy could see me, he never approached me. Whenever a ladies' choice dance was announced, Andy disappeared. His rejection wounded me, but I bandaged my soul, knowing another scar had formed.

*     *     *

# CHAPTER SEVEN—WORRY AND RESIGNATION

I was tucked safely in geography class when I heard the news. The principal, who rarely disturbed classes with P.A. announcements, cleared his throat and apologized in a stiff and formal tone for his interruption. "At approximately 12:30 p.m., President John Fitzgerald Kennedy, while riding in a motorcade in Dallas, Texas, was shot by an unknown assassin. I'm sorry to tell you, the President was pronounced dead at 1 p.m. after efforts to save his life failed. Details are still forthcoming, but I want to assure you that our government is still intact. School will dismiss at the usual time. Thank you."

A few girls burst into tears. Shocked, sober faces looked to Miss Gold for direction. "This is indeed a tragedy, but our country is strong," she said.

"Now the communists will take over," one girl declared.

"No, as you probably know, the vice president takes over the presidential duties," Miss Gold said. "Our government has contingency plans for such an event as this. Remember studying Abraham Lincoln's assassination? Who remembers his successor?"

The mute class stared through her. "Well, if I remember my history, it was a man named Andrew Johnson." She paused, lost in thought. "That's odd . . . our new president will be Lyndon Johnson."

While Miss Gold chattered about history and geography and shifted our attention from the tragedy, I tried to picture our young President dead. My parents, though Republicans, had admitted President Kennedy had done many good things for the country. Whenever the TV news programs aired snippets of the Kennedy clan, Mom paid attention to Jackie's outfits, and I watched John Jr. and Caroline romp playfully with their mom and dad. The First Family appeared so happy and alive that I couldn't alter the TV image to picture the President dead.

At the end of the period, I trudged to my next class and overheard snatches of conversations confessing fears for our country and the Kennedy family. Some students wept while others raged that the assassination was a communist plot to take over our country. I remembered the nuclear attack practice drills when I dived under my desk and feared war with the communists. Now, I didn't know what would happen.

Over the weekend, I stayed glued to the television. Footage of the assassination played countless times and burned a memory of horror in my mind. I watched a pale, dry-eyed Jackie witness Lyndon Johnson's swearing-in ceremony aboard the presidential plane, ninety minutes after her husband died. And Sunday, on live television, I watched

Jack Ruby kill Lee Harvey Oswald, Kennedy's alleged assassin. I couldn't believe what I saw. Nothing seemed real.

Also on that Sunday, television news reported that Jackie and the children accompanied the casket to the Capitol where the President would lie in state for mourners to bid their farewells. When John Jr. became restless in the Rotunda, he was taken to the Speaker's office where he saw a flag on the desk. "I want to take a flag home to my Daddy," he said. News cameras captured John Jr., a day shy of his third birthday, as he stood on the Capitol steps, one hand holding his mother's, the other hand clutching his tiny flag. Tears sprang to my eyes and drizzled my cheeks.

I looked at my dad, sitting in his favorite chair, bare feet propped on the hassock. He held a section of the Sunday Post-Dispatch, the remaining sections scattered like leaves around him. He caught me staring at him and took a sip of his Pepsi. The ice cubes rattled as he set the glass back on the table. He sucked on a sliver of ice and reached for a pretzel. "Something the matter?"

I wanted his assurance he wasn't going to die; instead, I replied, "It's so sad."

He munched a pretzel. "Yep."

Mom, who had been mending socks, looked up from her work and noticed my tear-streaked face. "Of course, it's sad. Some maniac shoots the President, and suddenly two small children are fatherless." She glanced at Dad, then back at me. She must have put two and two together because she patted the sofa cushion next to her. "Come here, sweetie."

I hopped onto the sofa, and Mom put an arm around me and wiped my tears with her rough hand.

"You don't have to worry. Dad and I aren't going to die," she said.

"Not today," Dad said, his eyes focused on his paper.

Mom gave a short laugh, but she frowned at him. "Your father means no one is going to shoot us. We hope you'll be all grown up when we die, but only God knows when that time will be." Mom hugged me and gave me a big smooch.

Dad glanced up, lifting one eyebrow. "Anything else I can do for you?"

He tried to be funny, so I smiled at him. "No." I sniffed.

"Did you hear the story about the bed?" He paused briefly and rubbed his bald head. "I haven't made it up yet." His grin made his blue eyes sparkle.

"Oh, Daddy, you've been telling that same joke for years."

He chuckled softly and returned to his reading.

That night, as I lay in bed and said my prayers, I prayed to God my parents wouldn't die and leave me alone. Who would want a red-skinned kid?

School was cancelled the next day because of the President's funeral. On television, the repetitious drum cadence made my ears throb. The dirge so saddened me that I left the house in search of my brother, whose company had to be more uplifting.

The next morning, the same as any other day, Mom woke me with a kiss. I shuffled into the kitchen where Dad greeted me in his usual manner. "Good morning glory."

I groaned and slid into my place at the table, across from my brother. The radio on the counter spewed forth the weather report, and Dad held up a finger to silence me, never missing a forkful as he listened to the report, I'm sure, for the umpteenth time. Mom plopped a plate of bacon and eggs in front of Roger and me and then hurried to fetch the toast, her robe stirring the air. The familiar routine soothed my weekend anguish.

When a peppy jingle replaced the dull weather report, I said good morning to Dad. Dressed in his work khakis and concrete-crusted boots, Dad finished his breakfast and drained his orange juice. I noticed his smooth hands and neatly trimmed nails, which looked as if he didn't do a lick of manual labor. But I knew he wore gloves. Mom's hands affirmed evidence of her work: painting walls, washing cars, cutting grass, scrubbing clothes, and cleaning house. In their hands, I saw the testimony of their work and their love. Hands that labored to shelter and clothe me also held and comforted me. Mom and Dad's mere physical presence brightened my gloomy mood. I realized how lucky I was to have two parents who cared for me—no matter what I looked like.

Eventually, students resumed a normal school routine where studies and activities replaced grief for a fallen president. Before long, Christmas break arrived. Over the holidays, I moped and cried, convinced I'd never have a boyfriend following Andy's snub. I mourned loss for something I never possessed. "In My Room" by the Beach Boys became my theme song. After my pity party wound to an end, I resigned myself to future spinsterhood, but I was determined not to have a dull life.

By New Year's, I had taken inventory, noted my good qualities, and decided I liked myself despite my imperfections. My birthmark, I believed, made me unique and unforgettable. Although I still didn't understand what caused it, I had learned to live with it. Recently though, I noticed two tiny bumps in the red area of my chest. I thought they were moles, except for their color, and Mom thought so too when I showed her.

We were in the bathroom across the hall from my bedroom. "Now, I know you think this is stupid, but we can at least try this," Mom said.

"It's just a wives' tale." I rolled my eyes and yanked up the strap of my A-cup bra.

"So what if it is? Maybe it works."

I shook my head. "No. I'm not letting you rub a potato on my warts. I should see a doctor."

"Look, if this doesn't work, you can see the doctor. You know how easily you bleed from your birthmark, and a doctor may not be able to help. You said your bra strap is rubbing on the bumps, so let's try this."

With a sigh, I slipped my strap aside. "All right, do your voodoo."

Mom cut the Idaho potato in two and rubbed both halves of the raw potato on my warts. "Okay, now I have to bury these." Mom headed for the door. "You better not wash the area for a little while," she yelled back.

"Why me?" I moaned to myself. Looking in the mirror, I saw potato juice dribbled on my chest and wanted to wash, but I heeded the voodoo woman's advice and repositioned my clothes. Mom learned all her tricks from Grandma. Supposedly, the recipient of the treatment must not know where the potato is buried, and once the potato rots, the warts should disappear.

Mom's potato wart cure wasn't any stranger than her treatment of sties. Whenever I detected a sty developing, Mom, using the band of her wedding ring, lightly traced the sign of the cross over the sty three times in succession. "Father, Son, Holy Spirit," she prayed. I prayed none of my friends would learn of Mom's superstitions and that God would forgive us.

While I waited for my warts to vanish, but generally satisfied with my overall appearance, I pledged to be a good student and a good person, and fill my life with things I enjoyed. If a boyfriend came along—fine. But, I refused to chase boys in desperation. They would have to accept me for what I was, not for what I looked like. After my appraisal, I didn't expect my life to change dramatically, yet, thanks to my parents, it did.

\*　　\*　　\*

# CHAPTER EIGHT—NEW CHALLENGES

Neither a dreary January nor the notion of future spinsterhood dampened my spirits when I returned to school after the holiday break. I told all my friends the exciting news.

My mom was expecting a baby.

I was thrilled when Mom told my brother and me about the baby. Having had little contact with pregnant women, I didn't know what to expect. I wondered what the new baby would look like. Would it be a boy or a girl? My brother hoped for a boy, but I just prayed the baby wouldn't be born with a birthmark.

I considered my last half of seventh grade "the months of expectation." I watched Mom's shape transform as she devised lists and collected supplies for the baby. She never really explained what was happening to her or what would occur, so I watched from the periphery and concentrated on my schoolwork.

I also kept one eye on my warts. One day, months after voodoo woman buried the potato in its secret spot, I discovered my warts were gone. I hadn't noticed them shrinking—they just disappeared. With a new respect for my mother's talents, I pondered my own abilities, dreamed of summer vacation, and awaited the arrival of my baby brother or sister.

From the time I was eight years old, I spent summers in the family pool that Dad's construction company had built in 1959. Located in the vacant lot between my cousins' house and ours, the Olympic-size pool was used by Dad's brothers and their children. My cousin Jo, the daughter of Dad's eldest brother who lived across town, spent every summer day at the pool. Just a year older than me, she had learned to swim at the public pool, and she had taught me how to do all the strokes, tread water, and dive. I taught my brother what I had learned.

When summer vacation began, I couldn't wait to spend my days swimming. I also wanted a new bike. I remembered Jo urging me to take an official swimming class and a life-saving course. While pondering my abilities, I decided to do just that.

I dragged my nine-year-old brother with me the first day of swimming lessons at the public pool. I shooed him into the boys' locker room and hurried through the girls' showers, catching up with him inside the pool area. Feeling naked in my one-piece swimsuit, I glared back at the kids who gawked at my birthmark as I guided my brother to the water.

"Okay, get in the water and swim across the pool," the swimming instructor bellowed.

Roger and I got in and swam across and back in the two-foot deep pool.

"You two," the instructor pointed to Roger and me, "move on down to the five-foot."

When we got to the five-foot end of the pool, the next instructor ordered us to swim across the pool. Roger and I did so.

The instructor pointed to the other section of the massive pool. "You two, go over to the six-foot."

When we got to the other side, the next instructor laughed at the two small people standing before him. "So, show me what you got," he snickered.

That side of the pool was wider than the previous section. I worried my brother wouldn't make it. "Do any stroke you want," I whispered to my brother before we jumped in. Although I finished before Roger, and he swam in a crooked line, he finished with a silly smile, water dripping from his crew cut.

The instructor shook his head. "Move all the way down to the twelve-foot."

I was getting pretty tired by that time. Luckily, the pool didn't go any deeper, so Roger and I ended up in the advanced class, the shortest and youngest swimmers in the class. I heard the whispers from my classmates about my red arm and back, but I ignored them, satisfied that I could swim better than anyone in the class.

Three weeks later, having finely tuned my swimming, I took the junior life-saving course and earned a red badge that

Mom sewed on my bathing suit. Roger couldn't wait until he was twelve and could take the course.

With one of my summer goals completed, I concentrated my attention on getting a new bike. I whined daily to my parents. Dad proposed I earn half the money for the bike and he'd kick in the rest.

After some thought, I decided to put my swimming talent to use by giving lessons. When I told a few neighborhood kids I would be teaching an hour and a half private swim lesson for $1.50, they quickly signed up, more interested in cooling off during the muggy summer days than in learning to swim. Word of the lessons spread faster than gossip on a party line. As my schedule filled, I fretted about the kids' first impression of a red and white swimming teacher. Only part of my redness showed when I wore clothes, but a swimsuit—a two-piece—would reveal much more.

The first day of my new endeavor, my swimsuit covered by a baggy tee shirt, I skimmed bugs from the pool while I waited for my first student. Right on time, a mother and her little tyke arrived.

After introductions, she dropped her child's swim bag, sank onto a lounge chair, and adjusted her sunglasses. "You don't mind if I stay and watch?" she asked. "Matthew would like that."

"Sure, fine with me," I said and pulled off my shirt. Matthew stepped back a pace and stared at my body, his message clear. I squatted down to his eye level and pointed to my arm. "This is my birthmark. It's kind of like a freckle but a different color."

"It sure is big," he said.

"Yes, but don't worry. It can't hurt you." I straightened up and held out my red hand, which he accepted. "Come on, let's get wet."

I slithered into the pool next to the ladder in the shallow end; the brisk water crept above the top of my suit. I dunked my shoulders under the water and hoped I wasn't shivering. "Come down the ladder," I told Matthew.

As he stepped onto the first ladder rung, the water ankle deep, he said, "Oh, it's cold," and hopped back out.

"It's a little chilly, but your body will adjust." I had no idea what I was saying—my feet were already numb. "Try it again."

Matthew dipped a foot in the water as if it were an icy lake. He shuddered and hauled himself back to the concrete deck. After he shook his arms and marched in place, he declared, "Okay, I'm ready." Once more he descended.

"Good, now doesn't it feel warmer?" I asked when he finally got to the third step.

"Uh-hum," he shivered.

"Come on Matthew, all the way," Matthew's mom shouted from her chair.

Matthew looked at his mom and then at me. He touched his toenail to the pool floor, his hands still gripping the ladder. He faced away from me with his body frozen to the rungs, the three and a half feet of water lapping his chin. I grasped his waist and said, "Good job. Now, I want you to let go, and I will hold you up."

The child's chin quivered, and he began to whimper and tremble. "I want to go home," he said, still clinging to his lifeline.

"You do as Debbie says," the mother yelled.

The child threw a beseeching look in her direction.

"Matthew, it's going to be fun learning to swim," I said. I had no idea how to pry the kid off the ladder, but then a thought struck me. "Climb back up, Matthew. Sit on the top step." He did so, now facing the pool instead of the deck. "Hold on tight and watch me."

When he was secure, I took off across the pool doing my best crawl. After a fancy turnaround against the wall, I swam the last few yards underwater and tickled Matthew's dangling feet before I surfaced in a flourish. "Ta-dah! See, you're going to learn to do that."

"W-w-wo-wow," he chattered.

"Okay, back in the pool."

After I coaxed and his mother threatened, Matthew allowed me to carry him through the water, although I wasn't much taller than he was. When I tried to get him to float, he thrashed and clawed like a wildcat. Trying to escape the water, he dug his feet into my thighs and hips and climbed me like a tree. He had a chokehold around my neck with one arm; his other hand squashed a handful of my swimsuit and a chunk of my skin. In my ear, he coughed and screamed, "No! No!"

It was the longest hour and a half wrestling match of my life. What had I gotten myself into? My body hurt everywhere, but visions of a new bike sustained me in battle.

Throughout the week, when I explained to my other students that I was born with a birthmark, they accepted my red skin better than my old classmates had. Getting them to listen became my challenge. Poolside time-outs and promises of free swim time kept the students in check during the lessons.

After the first week of teaching, I made a few changes. First, I scheduled the older children in the morning and moved the shivering younger kids to the warmer afternoons. Second, I enforced a new rule—no parents during the lesson. That decreased the clinging and crying. Finally, I added props, devices to aid the children with buoyancy and give them more confidence. Soon I developed a feel for pace and found my rhythm for teaching each student. While some kids were fearless, others were timid, and I learned to accept their differences. Often I learned more from the students than they learned from me.

I never realized that teaching swimming lessons was such hard work. The long days exhausted me, but a soak in a hot bath and a slathering of Mom's Avon Vita Moist revived me before dinner. I ate like a lumberjack, and, several evenings a week, I hurried off to drill team practice. The grueling days sped by, interrupted at times by a thunderstorm, which temporarily paused the swimming or marching.

Halfway through the summer of '64, my sister Diane was born. According to Mom, it was the event of the decade. She claimed she hadn't needed any pain medication, and she had watched the delivery in a mirror positioned above her. Afterwards, she had walked to the waiting room and told Dad they had a girl.

Baby Diane fascinated me—her tiny nails, pug nose, and wrinkly skin. She was perfect in every way—no birthmarks. "How did things go so wrong for me?" I asked myself. I wasn't exactly sure how babies were made or how they were born, yet my sister was here, and I loved her the moment I first saw her.

When Mom caught me staring at the baby in her bassinet, she said, "She looks just like you when you were born."

I hated to disagree with her, so I said nothing. I was happy my sister wouldn't have to suffer because she had a birthmark. I wondered what she would think of me when she grew up and noticed my difference.

Although my sister was a new and wonderful distraction, I still had obligations to my swimming students. When an occasional student excelled, I beamed with pride, and when students didn't do as well, I encouraged him or her to keep trying. Besides, there was always next year. By the end of summer, I had a dark tan, sun-bleached hair, a baby sister, and a new powder blue bike.

*    *    *

# CHAPTER NINE—A BOY LIKES ME

My preparation for spinsterhood (and a great and interesting life) was well underway during my eighth grade year. I threw myself into life and didn't care if boys were a part of it. My loyal girlfriends and I attended school activities, hung out after games at the Dairy Castle across from school, went to movies, and discussed everything at slumber parties. I escaped into Dr. Tom Dooley books and music of the Beach Boys. Baby sister demanded attention but enriched my life.

Although I got a D in music and my teacher advised me to stay away from musical instruments, I fiddled around with Dad's baritone ukulele. I picked my way over notes and taught myself a few chords. When I tired of the plunk-plunk sound of the four-string instrument, I begged Dad for a real guitar. He bought me a Stella, an inexpensive acoustic with a wide neck and unforgiving strings that crippled my fingertips. By the time I learned to play "Blowing in the

Wind," I had a new appreciation for the instrument and a callus on every fingertip.

After eighth grade graduation, I taught swimming lessons again, and my cousin Jo joined me in the adventure. Big-boned and blond, she swam like Esther Williams, her stroke so graceful she didn't disturb the water. She was easygoing and a good student in school. Having finished a straight-A freshman year of high school, she talked with me about teachers, classes, and activities. I couldn't wait to be a part of it. With the money I earned that summer, I bought contact lenses because I wanted to look my best, despite my birthmark.

At the end of summer, before I started high school, I discontinued my baton lessons and left the drill team, feeling too mature to parade down Main Street. I started taking guitar lessons. When it came time to choose my high school classes, I signed up for freshman chorus. What good was a guitar player who couldn't sing?

High school frightened me more than I dared admit. Memories of grade school taunts and junior high school rejections caused a twitter inside me. I wanted to be normal, but more importantly I wanted to feel accepted. I figured the best way for that to happen was to blend in with my peers, so I chose my fall wardrobe as if my survival depended on it.

More than four thousand students attended the school, increasing my terror and confusion. Finding the correct building, floor, and room number required a map, perseverance, and hustle.

My chorus class met in the basement of the cafeteria, a room decorated with simple wooden risers, an ebony grand piano, and a folding table. I squeezed onto a riser littered with a hodgepodge assortment of students and their stacks of books. Mr. Jackson, the teacher, a slender man with a receding hairline, methodically segregated the class into singing ranges—soprano, alto, tenor, and bass—according to our two-minute singing audition. I qualified as a soprano and practiced scales and exercises along with the class.

As I became more familiar with my school surroundings, my terror and confusion diminished. I didn't see much of my junior high friends, each with her customized curriculum, except during lunch or before or after school. Jane and Darla, my old baton buddies, had schedules similar to mine, so I spent more time with them; however, I met several new girls who seemed to like me. At least they didn't ridicule me for having a red arm.

A few weeks into the semester, a boy with dark hair and eyes approached me in the hallway outside my chorus class. "Hey, it's good to see you again," he said with a smile.

I didn't understand what he meant, but I smiled and said hello.

"How do you like chorus?" he asked, shifting his books to his other hip.

"So far, so good." I then realized he was in my class. "How about you?"

"It's okay, but I hope we start singing some real songs pretty soon. But, it beats study hall."

I cast glances at him as we walked along. He was a half a head taller than me and of average build. I suspected his hair was wavy, but he had it smoothed down with a short bang sweeping his forehead. Not one blemish marred his smooth complexion.

When we emerged from the building to go our separate ways, he said, "Well, I'll see you around," and he hastened away.

Glowing with expectation after my encounter, I headed for algebra class. Later during lunch, I saw the handsome fellow talking with a boy who belonged to my church youth group. "Good," I thought to myself, "I can find out from Dan who he is."

The following week, before chorus class, the boy once again sidled up to me in the hall. "Hi Jo, how's it going?"

I wasn't sure I heard him correctly. "Fine." I didn't know what to talk about, so I kept walking. Although I hadn't talked to Dan, I learned from roll call the boy's name was Alex. He strolled beside me in his polished penny loafers, permanent press slacks, and button-front shirt, looking as crisp as a newly-printed twenty-dollar bill. Finally, I asked, "How do you like your classes?"

His head erect, he stared down his nose at me. "They're okay. I was back East for a year . . . my dad's in the air force. School there was a little more advanced." As we entered the classroom, he said, "Wait for me after class. I want to ask you something."

"Sure." I smiled and watched him swagger across the room.

During class, I saw Alex glancing in my direction several times. When he caught me looking back, he smiled and nodded. I grinned and lowered my eyes, embarrassed he saw me. I wondered what he wanted to ask me. He seemed like a nice boy. As the class rehearsed "Moon River" for the twelfth time, my nerves tensed tighter with each note. At last, the bell rang, and the horde bolted out the door. I dawdled behind, gathering my belongings and composure when Alex approached.

"Hi," he said. "Thanks for waiting."

I looked into his brown eyes. "What did you want to ask me?"

"Well, I was wondering if you would go to the football game with me Friday night."

*He's asking me out.* I almost screamed.

I paused so long he added, "We can meet at the gate . . . watch the game . . . maybe go to the dance afterwards." He edged closer to me.

I tried to remain poised, but I wanted to throw my arms around him and thank him. "That sounds great. I'd love to go."

"Good. I'll meet you at 7:45 or so."

"Okay . . . thanks."

He gave me a grin. "I'll see you later then, Jo."

"Okay . . . bye." I felt like an idiot who couldn't put two words together. What was Jo—some kind of Eastern greeting? Although I didn't understand, I was so thrilled a boy took interest in me that I practically skipped to class.

While my algebra teacher droned on about *x* and *y*, a million thoughts raced through my head. *I had a date* led the pack, followed by *a boy likes me,* and *my birthmark didn't offend him. I can't wait to tell my friends, my parents—uh-oh, maybe I should have asked permission. My parents had never discussed dating with me—not that the issue had come up. Well, it wasn't as if I were going anywhere with him, except to a school function. I'm sure my folks will agree. Oh gosh, what will I wear? Slacks are against the school's dress code, so that leaves a skirt—yes—my new maroon one to show my school spirit. And I'll need a sweater at night. Oh, I hope I have knee socks to match my skirt. Are my saddle oxfords polished? I can't wait to tell Jane and Darla. I hope . . .*

A ringing bell interrupted my thoughts. Hastily, I scribbled the homework assignment from the board and dashed to lunch. I quickly spilled the news to my friends.

"I don't know who he is," Jane complained.

"Me neither," said Darla. "Point him out when you see him."

"For sure you'll see him at the football game and dance," I said. "Oh look, there's Dan. I've got to talk to him. Be back in a flash."

I hurried over to speak to Dan. "I didn't know you knew Alex," I said to him.

"Yeah, we're old friends," he said. "I knew him when he went to North."

"North Junior High?"

"Yeah, seventh grade. Why, what's up?"

"He asked me to go to the football game with him."

"Great. Have a nice time." He slurped the last of his drink.

"Thanks Dan. See ya later."

Back with the girls, I reported, "Dan said Alex went to North."

"So did I," Darla said. "I don't remember him."

"Alex keeps saying, 'Hi Jo' and 'Bye Jo,' and I thought it was a greeting." I propped an elbow on the table and leaned my head against my hand. "You know, my cousin Jo went to North. She's a year older than me. You don't suppose he thinks I'm her?"

"You both have the same last name," Jane pointed out. "And, the same color hair and eyes."

My head snapped up. "Oh no! I have a date with someone who thinks I'm somebody else!"

"It's better than no date." Darla snorted back a laugh.

"What should I do?"

"Tell him," both girls yelled at the same time.

"This is bizarre," I mumbled.

My parents gave their consent for me to attend the game and the dance with Alex. By Friday, I still hadn't found the courage to tell Alex my name. All through the football game, I tried to think of an opening, but I was afraid to confess. I enjoyed having him sit close to me, smile at me, talk to me. If I told him I wasn't Jo, maybe he would call off the date.

The Belleville Maroons won the football game. Maroon and white confetti sailed through the air, sprinkling us like snowflakes. Hand in hand, Alex and I merged with the crowd of jubilant students heading for the gym and the victory celebration. My heart hammered with each step.

Inside the gym, decorations of maroon and white draped the walls. A live rock band, amplifiers at high volume, deafened the first dancers on the floor.

Alex pulled me toward the middle of the dance floor. "Come on, Jo, let's dance."

"My name is Debbie."

He pointed to his ear and screamed over the music. "What? I can't hear you."

I moved closer to him and spoke louder. "My name is Debbie."

A look of confusion crossed his face, but he smiled and started dancing. I joined him, thinking that later, we would sort it out—when there was a pause in the music.

\*     \*     \*

# CHAPTER TEN—METAMORPHOSIS

In the midst of transformation, only the heartiest leaves withstood the tides of the autumn winds. Liberated by the currents, fragile leaves, toasted red and orange, fluttered to the earth where they withered and moldered. Mom said she hated autumn because everything died. Enthralled with Alex, I never noticed the metamorphosis occurring.

I finally confessed to Alex I wasn't who he thought I was. "My cousin, Jo, is a year older than me. *She* went to North with you, not me. If you want, I can introduce you." I gave him an out, but he just laughed at my suggestion. When he gave me a friendly hug, I knew he liked me.

Alex, the considerate boyfriend, escorted me to my classes as time and distance allowed, telephoned me in the evenings, and arranged for dates—football games, dances, and get-togethers with friends. He treated me with respect and kindness that I had never expected from a boy. After suffering boys' taunts and rejections most of my life, Alex's refreshment assuaged my hunger for male acceptance and validated my worth as a female. Although I had convinced myself I could be happy without a boyfriend, Alex's attention changed my perspective.

I relished Alex's kindness, feeling special because of the closeness between us. While I had many boy friends in my neighborhood, they only cared that I could play ball, shoot a BB gun, and climb a tree. They didn't see me as a girl. Alex made me feel like a girlfriend, the way he stared into my eyes, took my hand, or draped an arm around me. His behavior toward me seemed as natural for him as swimming was for me. He told me he had girlfriends when he lived back East. Despite his experience, he didn't rush the relationship.

While I appreciated Alex's gentlemanly ways, I wondered if and when he would kiss me. If he saw past my birthmark, would he see me as someone he wanted to kiss? I had no idea how to kiss a boy. In movies, the kissing scenes appeared so urgent and intense, almost brutal. Was actual kissing like that? I wasn't sure I was ready for it, but, just in case, I practiced kissing my hand, my mirror, and my floppy stuffed dog. Thankfully, my brother didn't catch me and tease the heck out of me.

When my church youth group planned a hayride around Halloween, I invited Alex. The group, couples and singles, met at a golf course where the bright lights dispelled the darkness. I spied Alex and hurried over. "I see you brought a blanket," I said, smiling.

He flashed a mischievous grin. "Yes, it might get chilly." He motioned to the hay wagon. "Let's get a spot."

The one-sided flatbed, loaded with a mound of loose straw, was hitched to a weathered tractor. Laughing like little children, Alex and I leaped on the wagon and nestled into the scratchy straw. The mixed scents of grain, earth, and grass in the hay tickled my nose. The rest of the group boarded and got situated but not without flinging handfuls of straw at one another.

A grizzled man in a plaid jacket adjusted his ball cap and fired up the tractor. With a sudden jerk, we were underway. The driver made a wide semicircle around the lighted golf course. A worn, oiled road divided a line of tall trees that edged the fairways from the cornfields that stretched into the black night. The tractor crawled slowly along the wavy road as crickets, frogs, and owls serenaded us. Boys hopped off the wagon to avoid flying straw and then jumped back on, tackling girls and burying them with hay. Wrapped in blankets, couples cuddled, their muffled words and sounds mingling with the hum of the tractor. The youthful chaperones ignored the horseplay and wooing, content in their own world.

Alex sat beside me, one arm around me, our legs dangling over the side of the wagon. As we talked, I tried not to feel self-conscious about what was going on around me. Soon the wagon passed beyond the illuminated golf course, and only the dim tractor headlights lit the way. Stars twinkled overhead, and I saw the moon full and waiting.

One minute I was talking to Alex and then, suddenly, his mouth closed over mine, silencing my words. His lips were soft and gentle, drawing me into the moment. I recalled thinking "I'm getting kissed" before my mind released all thought. I closed my eyes and floated with the sensation. Alex's lips parted as they tasted mine, and something fluttered inside me. My heart galloped, and my breathing ceased. He slowly pulled away, and I opened my eyes like Sleeping Beauty. His face remained inches from mine, his eyes reading my reaction.

I met his penetrating gaze and answered him with a smile. My chest heaved when I drew in a breath. "Mmm," I purred like a contented cat.

"I've wanted to do that for some time," he said, still close to my face.

"It was nice." The sound of my soft voice surprised me.

Because the night had a bite of winter in the wind, Alex unfurled the blanket and draped it around our shoulders. He tilted his head to the side, and his lips again sought mine. This time I was prepared and inhaled a breath as if I were diving underwater. His mouth moved unhurried, and I felt his free arm slide around my back. He pulled me closer. My arms embraced him as if they had minds of their own. When his tongue parted my lips, I responded by instinct. Neither "Spin the Bottle" nor kissing my stuffed dog had trained me properly. Alex's soft exhalation warmed my cheek, and I figured it was okay to breathe through my nose while we kissed. After all, he was the experienced one.

When the lights of the golf course washed over us, Alex and I moved apart. The tractor stopped in the parking lot, and the passengers, more subdued, alighted. I hugged Alex one last time before we went our separate ways.

Just a few weeks remained until the school's traditional Thanksgiving Day football game against its rival, the East Side Flyers. The preceding day, deemed "Grundy Day" back in 1929, evolved into "Hobo Day," the best day of the school year. Relaxing the rigid dress code for one day, the administration allowed students to dress in ragged creations, preferably in maroon and white. School dismissed at noon for the Hobo Day parade, which began on Main Street in front of the school and terminated at the public square, twenty-one blocks east.

Belleville enjoyed its parades—Memorial Day, Veteran's Day, Santa Claus, Clean Up, Paint Up, Fix Up, and even Hobo Day. The Hobo Day parade not only energized the football team but also the city, most of whose residents were school alumni. For the parade, each class entered a float to be judged and the winner announced on the courthouse steps at the square. Last year's graduating class won best float four years in a row, setting a school record. This year's float theme was "Slogans," and my freshman class decided on "The Early Bird Catches the Worm."

Weeks before Thanksgiving, my class labored evenings and weekends to construct our float in an empty building at the stove foundry. First, the boys, especially those in shop, built two frames as the bodies of the bird and the worm and then covered the frames with chicken wire molded into the animals' shapes. While some students folded and fluffed crepe paper flowers, others attached them to the wire.

The tedious work and design problems taught us students to work together; moreover, we built friendships. I loved working on the float—the camaraderie, the discussions, and the flirtations. I met interesting new girls and boys, and since Alex wasn't much of a participant in the activities, we began to veer in opposite directions. Brian, one of the boys on student council, patrolled the work site like a politician. His blond hair, good looks, and winsome smile charmed me and every girl who eyed him. And everyone noticed Brian's group of prankster friends from Crest Mountain School, whose enthusiasm for frivolity interfered with the work. But eventually the float took shape.

By Thanksgiving week, as if influenced by the change of seasons, Alex and my romance degenerated. No harsh words had been exchanged; no declarations of conclusion had been announced. We simply lost interest in each other and moved apart. I wasn't sad because Alex proved to me I was likeable and worthy of a boy's affection. Working on the float, building new friendships, learning the guitar, and even pledging a sorority occupied my time. I felt good about myself.

When Hobo Day finally arrived, I donned a pair of worn jeans and rolled up the legs to below my knees. I put on one of Dad's old white shirts, knotted the tails around my waist, tied on my Keds, grabbed a heavy maroon flannel shirt, and set off for school. Anticipation of the parade consumed the morning. Nell, a girl with reddish blond hair and green eyes who sat in front of me in algebra class, showed up in her usual Weejuns and jeans that looked brand new. I gathered her family was well off because she lived in the more affluent section of town. Despite our sociological difference, we had become friends.

"Meet me after lunch in front of the auditorium," Nell said. "We can walk together in the parade."

"Cool. I'll tell Jane and Darla," I said.

"Helen and Susan will meet us, too."

"Fine. Do you think our float will arrive in one piece?"

"I heard they had some problems late last night as they were moving it out of the building, but I haven't heard anything more about it," she said.

"I just hope it stays together during the parade."

"Me too," Nell said.

After lunch, I met up with my friends. A sea of students clad in maroon and white mobbed Main Street in front of the school as the parade assembled. The homecoming court, football players, and cheerleaders balanced from seats of honor in maroon convertibles. Sounds of the band members tuning their instruments mixed with the cacophony of students yelling commands. My class gathered behind our float, last in the parade order. The group of Crest Mountain boys was wedged in the bed of the pickup truck hitched to tow the float. I was happy to see the flowers still attached to the giant bird and worm, but I noticed the other classes had constructed football players on their floats, not animals.

By the time the freshman float got to the square, the flowered bird's head dangled to the side like a stroke victim. The goal posts, a last minute addition, listed precariously forward. I heard the guffaws from the upper classmen. "A bird? Why didn't they build a football player?"

During the pep rally, the senior float was judged the best. My class, the laughing stock of the school, shambled off behind our crumbling creation.

The mighty Maroons lost the Thanksgiving Day football game by one point and forfeited the coveted trophy. At the float-burning ceremony the day after Thanksgiving, not much was left of the freshman float to dismantle. Like my relationship, it just fell apart, unable to withstand the tides.

\*     \*     \*

# CHAPTER ELEVEN—NEW BEGINNINGS

For more than a half century, my high school faithfully served the community where thousands of students had graduated. Besides the original structures, additions of a science library and a cafeteria could not contain the growing student population. The 1966-'67 school year made history when a second public high school opened on the east side of town. It was appropriately named Belleville Township High School East (BTHS East), and its creation not only divided my class but also the community.

Illinois Street separated the city into east and west halves. I counted myself lucky my close friends lived in the west half with me. Alex and Dan, half of my junior high class, and my cousin Jo lived on the east side of town. The school board sympathized with the seniors and decided they could finish their fourth year on the BTHS West campus. It was a year of comparisons between a new school that set precedents and an old school that followed tradition.

Shortly before my sophomore school year began, a girl from my old drill team contacted me about auditions for a group that was forming to complement the marching band. For lack of a better term, the band instructor (everyone called him Russ) referred to the group as the "Flag and Shield Girls." One of fourteen girls selected for the group, I traded my baton for a flagpole, as did Jane and Darla. My new friends, Nell and Susan, and my old friend Connie from junior high school were picked for the shield group.

Marching band replaced P.E. in my school schedule, but the practices provided me with plenty of exercise. While the band musicians practiced arrangements, the Flag and Shield Girls developed routines. After school, the entire band stomped around the football field and exacted drills in preparation for our first performance at the season-opener football game.

The night of our debut, I primped along with the other Flag and Shield Girls while we waited for the band director's cue. "How are we supposed to wear this?" I asked Darla, holding my tam, a flat knit cap with circular maroon stripes and a fluffy white pompom.

"I'm not sure, but we should be uniform," Darla said as she tested the tam in various positions atop her light brown hair.

"Uniform," Jane said with a laugh. "You call these uniforms?"

I looked at the girls around me. "Well, it's the best we could do on our meager budget. I know we don't look as flashy as we did in the drill team, but we don't look *that* bad."

"At least we won't be cold." Jane grumbled and tugged on her heavy white sweater.

"I kind of like the outfits," Darla said. "Besides, what could be more comfortable than sweaters, shorts, and tennis shoes?"

Jane brushed lint from her maroon corduroy shorts. "Yeah, I suppose you're right." Her smile revealed a mouth of metal.

"How does this look?" Darla asked and turned to face me. The tam sat askew on her smooth flip hairstyle.

Jane and I laughed. "Actually it looks okay," I said. "Well, maybe a little more forward." I tugged on her tam.

Nell, new to the marching scene, rushed over as we were securing our tams. "Oh, I hope I remember everything." She fidgeted with a strawberry curl. "Susan is making me so nervous."

"I know what you mean." I had been listening to Susan chatter like an auctioneer. "But, everything will be fine. Just don't forget to smile."

"I'll probably be too frightened," Nell said.

"Don't worry," Jane said, "nobody will be watching us anyway. Everyone will be watching Bruce or the majorettes."

Darla and I giggled. "He sure puts on a show," Darla said.

"Girls, it's time to line up," Russ yelled. "Is everyone ready?"

"Yes," a chorus answered with enthusiasm.

Halos blazed around the stadium lights, and fingers of brightness shimmered off the band's buffed instruments. Crunched in back of the goal posts, the band's eighty members stretched their ranks almost the width of the football field. In front of the band, I stood in line behind the girls holding shields, each with a letter that spelled Maroons. The small flag attached to my pole barely fluttered in the windless night. Out front in their skimpy outfits, the majorettes arranged themselves behind Bruce, the drum major. Russ paced nearby.

At Russ's signal, music erupted from the band, and Bruce pranced onto the field, leading into formations the majorettes, the shield girls, the flag girls, and the band. I smiled like a Hollywood star and weaved in and out, parading back and forth to the lively march. Somewhere in the stands, my parents watched me twirl my flagpole.

The routine progressed smoothly. When the music ended, the group had formed into columns from midfield to the goal line. Russ carried a short ladder to the fifty-yard line and climbed up. All eyes trained on him as he raised his baton. Band members snapped their instruments to the up and ready positions. Russ nodded his head and swung the baton into action. Behind me, drums rolled and the band began to play "The Star Spangled Banner." The crowd joined together in song. At the end of the opening, Russ grabbed his ladder, and with a bow-legged wobble, he headed for the sidelines. The band reversed direction and headed off the field while the football players were introduced.

Seated in the visitor section until the half-time performance, the band played sound effects, peppy tunes, and the school song during the game. Between the musical infusions, the band cheered for the team.

"Come on, Ref!" I heard a boy shout. "That's holding!"

I looked over my shoulder to see who yelled. A boy, his red hair peeking from beneath his band cap, grumbled about the call.

A minute later, I heard him cry, "Are you blind?" I turned and saw him leap to his feet and wave his trumpet in the air. "Give me a break here!" he said. "That's interference!"

"He sure is passionate," Darla whispered to me.

As the last seconds of the first half ticked off the game clock, the band assembled once again behind the end zone. At the buzzer, the football team sprinted to the locker room to regroup, and the band took the field.

The crowd applauded the half-time performance, but the cheerleaders scowled at us girls and then whispered among themselves. No one smiled. Based on their reception of us, I wondered if a school steeped in tradition would ever welcome innovation. Surrounded by convention, I felt excited to be part of something new just like the students at East, who were starting fresh, devising their own particular rituals.

Besides my participation in a new group, I made a new friend my sophomore year. A petite girl who sat across the aisle from me in German class aroused my interest with her lilting voice and infectious giggle. Before long, Gina and I were new best friends.

"What do you think about going to the sophomore boy's basketball game?" I asked Gina one winter day. She thought for a moment, then quickly bowed over her desk and slapped its top. Sitting up again, she threw back her chin-length brown hair and giggled, her braces sparkling like her blue-green eyes. "I don't know much about basketball . . . but why not?"

"Great," I said. "It'll give us something to do. Besides, we can check out the guys."

Gina giggled again, her laugh like music.

We met up after school at the gym and went inside. Except for a sprinkling of parents and a group of boy spectators, Gina and I were the only girls in attendance. "Where should we sit?" I asked Gina as my eyes swept the nearly vacant gym.

Gina nodded toward the bleachers beneath one of the baskets. "Let's sit over there."

Our loafers clicked on the hardwood floor as we made our way to our seats. Feeling the boys' scrutiny, Gina and I hastily sat down. "Well, I thought there'd be more people here," I whispered to Gina.

"Me, too," Gina said. "It's so quiet in here." She arranged herself on the worn bench and laid her Ainé purse aside.

When the game got underway, we clapped for the team, drawing a few looks in our direction. The coach, also my English teacher, shouted instructions to the players. Except for the coach's voice, the squeak of tennis shoes on the court, and an occasional groan, the game progressed like a silent movie.

"Okay, let's pick out our new boyfriends." I teased. "Which one do you like?"

"I don't know."

"I think that one is pretty cute." I indicated a lanky boy with a wave of dark hair hiding half his forehead. His brown eyes stayed riveted on the basketball as he loped up and down the court. "What do you think?"

Gina shrugged and smiled. "He's okay, I suppose."

"Oh, there's Brian on the bench. He's gorgeous," I sighed and stared at him.

By the end of the game, Gina and I had perused the team and dissected the boys as if they were our biology frogs. We escaped amid giggles but pledged to return.

After we had watched several games, the lanky basketball player appealed to me more and more. I couldn't stop thinking about him, and I hadn't even met him. When I confessed my feelings to Gina, she said, "Oh, that's Mark," as if she knew his name all along.

"You know him?" I asked.

She looked down. "We've kind of been talking."

"You—what?" The words shot from my mouth before I could soothe my hurt.

"Yeah, we've been talking," she said softly.

I quickly recovered. "Wow! That's neat! Really great."

Gina smiled. "Well, we'll see what happens."

"Ask him if he has any friends," I said with a laugh, thinking of Brian. He would be someone I would like to know.

Eventually I met Mark. With a tinge of pride, Gina introduced us, her eyes shining. A Crest Mountain School graduate, Mark was one of the pranksters in Brian's crowd. Since I first laid eyes on Brian, the cutest boy at the float building, I had fantasized about him. But I felt like a beggar at the foot of a god whenever he was near me. A popular, handsome boy like Brian would never look twice at someone who looked like me. It was a one-sided infatuation and a hopeless situation. Tradition (and Emily Post) dictated the girl wait for an introduction and wait for a boy's invitation to a social function. Wanting to set precedents like BTHS East and encouraged by my friends, I would recklessly defy convention when I asked Brian for a date.

*     *     *

# CHAPTER TWELVE—IT'S A DATE

A couple months later, on an April day, I lunched with my girlfriends in the school cafeteria and bemoaned my situation. "What will I say?"

"Just ask him," my best friend Gina said.

"I know he'll say, 'No.'"

"You won't know until you ask him," Nell chimed in as she shook one of her strawberry pigtails off her shoulder.

I munched my sandwich and looked across the crowded room. Brian, Mark, and the Crest Mountain crowd bantered loudly, oblivious to everyone around them, especially to the serious discussion at my table.

Jane caught me staring and said, "Don't just think about it. Do it . . . today."

"At least you'll know one way or another," Darla agreed with Jane, her old baton buddy.

I continued to stare. Where did my self-confidence go? I could march onto a football field in front of a crowd, but I couldn't find the courage to talk to Brian. I feared rejection because I had a red arm. For some months, I'd given Brian shy but interested smiles. Whenever I had looked his way, he'd smiled as if it were an automatic reaction, but his glance had ricocheted off me. Eventually, he had taken conscious notice of me, but the interplay had gone on for weeks before I had braved speaking to him, exchanging a few words with him.

Gina and Mark had been getting chummy since basketball season. She often approached Mark when he was surrounded by his pack of friends, which included Brian. I stayed glued to Gina's side, hoping by chance Brian would take more notice of me. I hoped . . .

Gina interrupted my thoughts. "Did you know he got his driver's license?"

"Yes. But *if* he says he'll go with me, should I expect him to drive to St. Louis? No parent would let their kid drive to St. Louis so soon after getting their license."

"He's a guy," Darla said. "Parents are easier on them. I should know . . . two brothers, remember?"

"First I have to get past asking him." I crumpled up my trash and stuffed it into my empty paper cup, preparing to chuck it in the can.

For days, I had rehearsed my invitation to Brian and sweated through each imagined scenario. I prayed his rejection would be swift and gentle.

Among a throng of students clogging the quadrangle, I spotted Brian ambling in my direction. For once, he was alone. I watched his steady pace and admired his prep-school look—nice slacks, collared shirt, and loafers. He wore his blond hair short and neatly combed. Occasionally, he nodded to passing acquaintances.

Before I intercepted him, I took a deep breath and remembered to be enthusiastic. "Hi, Brian. How are you?" I stopped in front of him and tightened the grip on my books to keep from shaking.

He stopped walking and smiled. "Fine. And you?"

"Oh, good," I said, my mouth suddenly dry. "Well, I was wondering . . . well . . . my sorority . . . KZX . . . is having a formal dance in a few weeks . . . on a boat on the river." Brian patiently listened to my ineloquent recitation. I garnered what little bravado I had left and continued. "Well, all the girls are inviting someone . . . so . . . I was hoping you might like to go with me." There! I got it out.

Brian's blue eyes drifted from my face. "Thank you for asking me."

*Uh-oh. He's searching for an excuse.* I quickly rambled on. "We can catch a ride to St. Louis with one of the older sorority girls, so transportation won't be a problem."

Brian's eyes returned to me, but his face did not betray his feelings. "I should probably get permission from my folks," he said. "When did you say it was?"

I told him the date.

"I'll let you know tomorrow," he said as unruffled as a brood hen.

"Sure, that would be great." I smiled sweetly. "Thanks."

He started off. "I have to get going, but I'll talk to you tomorrow."

"Okay, see you later." I hurried in the opposite direction, wanting to sprint.

I felt like a fool. Who was I to ask the most popular boy in class to go on a date? I was way out of my league. When I extended my invitation to Brian, I didn't see revulsion in his face or disdain in his demeanor, but I also didn't see eagerness. His manners impeccable, he handled my awkwardness with grace. I asked for the moon—formal attire, flowers, and a twenty-five mile trip to St. Louis. It was more than a date to Dodo Burger. I wouldn't be surprised if he said no. He barely knew me.

That evening, I tried to concentrate on my homework, but thoughts of Brian filled my head. What was he thinking? What would he say? At least he hadn't declined right away. That was a good sign. Perhaps, I should have asked someone else. Who? Boys weren't swarming around me to offer dates, except for the two freshmen I knew from band. One boy followed me like a puppy, and I didn't even know his name. The other boy, the red-haired trumpet player, was a downright pest. His name was Bobby, and he also graduated from Crest Mountain School. With a reputation for mischief, he flirted with every girl he saw and annoyed me. Since neither boy could drive and neither appealed to me in a romantic way, I never considered asking them to go with me to the dance. Besides, they were freshmen.

After a fitful night's sleep, I awoke early to allow myself plenty of time to choose an outfit. I rejected all the homemade skirts and dresses Mom had sewn for me in favor of an off-the-rack skirt and blouse. Lately, I noticed Mom's sewing wasn't up to her usual standards. The hemlines slanted down on my right side. I didn't want to complain, but I wanted to look my best for Brian. In the full-length hall mirror, I examined myself from every angle. "Hmm, this skirt hangs crooked, too," I thought. "Well, it will have to do." I hiked up the right side of my skirt and hurried on my way.

I fidgeted in my classes, checked my appearance in every bathroom mirror between classes, and counted the minutes before my rendezvous with Brian.

"You look fine," Gina told me after German class. "Quit worrying and get going." She gave me a gentle nudge.

"Okay. Okay." I threaded my way through the crowd. "He can only say no," I told myself. "He's too well-bred to ridicule me, so stop agonizing."

I spied Brian loitering next to the fountain in the middle of the quadrangle. I slipped into my bubbly Debbie persona, and with a springy step and a broad smile, I walked up to him as if I expected good news.

I noticed Brian watching me weave through the crowd of students toward him. His relaxed pose calmed my jitters. "How are you?" he asked.

"Great! I just found out I passed my German test." I gave a short laugh. "If I have to conjugate one more verb, I'll scream." I shook my head and reined in my blathering.

Brian smiled at me. "I checked with my parents about the dance." He didn't any waste time getting to the purpose of our meeting. I held my breath. "They said it was okay for me to drive us."

Oh, my goodness. He said *us*. I was so excited I could hardly stand still. "Really?" I asked, surprised.

"Yes. I wasn't sure they'd let me drive, but they agreed." He straightened his posture.

"That's great! Have you ever driven to St. Louis?"

"Not yet." He grinned and his blue eyes twinkled. "Will that be okay with your folks?"

"I certainly hope so." I smiled.

For the rest of the week, I floated three feet above the ground. My parents, though reluctant at first, were allowing me to ride with Brian.

Mom orchestrated a search to find the right dress for me. The choices of spring formals did not include gowns with long sleeves or turtlenecks. Most had plunging necklines, open backs, or spaghetti straps. I pawed through the racks of dresses. "I can't wear these," I moaned. A low-cut neckline would display the purple half of my chest and cleavage, and any backless option would reveal the irregular patches of red on my back.

"Don't worry. We'll find something," Mom said as she hunted through the selections.

I settled on a sleeveless white gown with an empire waist and a modest neck that provided the most cleavage and back coverage. Then I chose a short jacket that would cover my red arm. I found that exposing one colorful section of skin at a time diminished the shock for viewers. But eventually I would remove the jacket at the dance, so I devoted the next few weeks to sunbathing to darken my white skin and decrease the contrasting skin colors.

Meanwhile, Mom scheduled me for a hair appointment, and we searched for shoes and a purse. By the time we were finished shopping, I hated my body again. I hated that I was limited to certain styles, which weren't in style at all. I hated that my feet were so narrow I had trouble finding shoes. What was I thinking?

A couple weeks before the formal dance, Brian asked me out on a date. I couldn't have been more surprised. Whenever we saw each other at school, we barely said three words to each other.

Brian arrived at my house driving a white, 1966 T-Bird, and he impressed my parents with his polite manners. We went to a movie at the new cinema and then to dinner at the finest restaurant in town. Afterwards, he drove me home and walked me to the door. Although I hesitated and hoped for a kiss, Brian told me he enjoyed the evening and left.

I didn't know what to think. Was he interested in me, or was he simply being kind? Our conversation had flowed smoothly without any awkward pauses, and we had laughed about similar problems at school. When I had looked at him, I didn't see desire in his eyes or feel his attraction for me. I had to settle for his charm and kindness and friendship.

On the evening of the formal, the intermittent rain showers flattened my hairdo but didn't dampen my spirits. Mom fussed over me as if I were performing in another recital. Dad took notice but sat on the sidelines, pretending to read his paper, and said nothing. Stumbling around in my heels, hoping I wouldn't twist an ankle, I fretted over every detail.

Brian arrived with a corsage for me and polite greetings for my parents. Mom folded back my jacket and pinned the corsage to my dress for all to admire. After the small talk, I bade my parents a hasty good-bye.

Huddled beneath an umbrella, Brian and I glided to his glistening car. "You look nice," he said.

"You don't look so bad yourself," I teased, taking in his striking figure in his white tuxedo jacket and dark slacks. He looked positively gorgeous, my own James Bond, if only for a night. Like a proper gentleman, he opened my door and helped me gather my dress into the car, then drove like my grandma away from the house. A half hour later, we crossed the Poplar Street Bridge over the Mississippi River into Missouri. Fortunately, Brian didn't get lost en route to the riverfront. He spotted the boat and guided the car onto the sloping cobblestone bank. The rain continued at a slow pace.

He parked the car. "I'll come around with the umbrella."

Wanting to keep my dress dry, I yanked up my skirt, ducked under the umbrella, and took Brian's arm. We slowly sidestepped toward the gangway across the two-inch gaps between the wet cobblestones.

"I can't walk in heels on these cobblestones." Laughing, I wobbled and clung tighter to Brian, who was laughing with me. "I hope we don't end up in the river." I negotiated the slippery descent without wedging my heel in a gap or twisting my ankle.

The boat rocked ever so slightly at its mooring as we stepped aboard. Brian found us a table next to a window level with the water line. After introductions, the band started playing, and the boat departed down river, leaving behind the lights of St. Louis shimmering in the rain.

Although the evening's enchantment dazzled me, my prince was absent. However, my friend Brian made my fairy tale come true—if only for one night. I wondered when my true prince would arrive to make my dream a reality, not caring that I was different.

\*　　\*　　\*

# CHAPTER THIRTEEN—PREVIEWS AND REVIEWS

Peace . . . love . . . flower children.

In 1967, teens either joined the hippie counterculture or tried to emulate them within the confines of parental control. Like the later group, I was no different. I grew my hair long and sang about going to San Francisco and wearing flowers in my hair.

Summer days found me once again at the pool teaching swimming lessons. Summer evenings, I put on my frayed, cut-off jeans, a white t-shirt, and a pair of rubber thongs and cruised Main Street with Gina, Jane, or Nell taking turns as chauffeurs. It was nice having girlfriends who could drive, but I couldn't wait for my birthday so I could get my license. It didn't matter that the Impala or Nova or Wildcat belonged to our parents; we had wheels. Nell had the coolest car—a '65 olive-green Mustang—that her parents allowed her to drive to school.

On weekends, my friends and I hung out at my pool, often in the company of Bobby, the pest, and his friend Gregg. Bobby professed his love for me, and I ignored him. Later, the girls and I cruised around town to find a street dance where the bands were as hot as the summer nights. I savored every minute of my freedom.

Besides being obsessed with driving, my girlfriends and I participated in school-related summer activities. Each year, the junior class wrote and then performed a musical play for an event called the Junior Jam. My friends and I offered our creative insights, considering scenes, plot, roles, and music. I faithfully practiced my singing and guitar playing and hoped to audition for a part. Meanwhile, those of us in the Flag and Shield Girls rehearsed new routines for band. Russ planned to introduce pom-poms into the halftime performance, which I knew would really tick-off the cheerleaders.

As the start of school neared, I modeled my recently purchased fall outfits one day while Grandma was visiting. "How do you like this one?" I asked her, twirling in circles so she could see my green suit. "I have matching tights and a brown turtleneck to wear with it."

"Very nice," she said as she studied me.

Mom finished rinsing dishes and dried her hands. "I told her I would sew her some new clothes, but she insisted on getting store-bought with her swimming money."

I shrugged out of the coat. It was too hot to try on wool. "You know you can't make jackets or slacks."

Mom grabbed the coat from me and hung it on a hanger. "I know, but you could let me make you some new skirts."

"Nothin' wrong with homemade," Grandma agreed, nodding and rocking slightly in the stationary kitchen chair.

"No, but something must be wrong with Mom's tape measure," I said. "The last several skirts she made me were lopsided."

Mom went to the closet, returning quickly with her tape measure. "I measured twice." She pointed to my crooked hemline. "Look at that skirt. That's from the store."

"Looks off to me," Grandma said.

I leaned from side to side, trying to see where the hemline fell. "It's probably because of my fat leg."

"What fat leg?" Grandma asked.

I pulled up the knee-length skirt and pointed to my left leg. "This leg is fatter than my right." I turned sideways, so they could see the depression along the side of my right thigh.

Grandma bent over for a closer look, and then sat up and shook her head "If that don't beat all."

"I think this is a muscle . . . from all my marching," I said as I rubbed the dent of the thinner leg.

"On just one leg?" Mom unfurled her faded yellow tape. "Let me measure something. Drop the skirt back down." She kneeled in front of me, placing one end of the tape at my waist. She stretched the tape to my right knee. "Twenty inches," she announced and moved the tape to my left side. "Twenty-one inches." She looked up at me. "That can't be right." She measured again. "Yep. It's the same— different by an inch."

"She's just like me—crooked," Grandma said.

"Oh, Mom," my mother chided and stood up.

Grandma wagged her finger at me. "Did I ever tell you how I ended up crooked?" She didn't wait for my answer. "I was in a pond, riding on the shoulders of some boy. He stumbled and pitched me forward." She tilted forward in her chair. "I went headfirst into the water, and my head stuck straight down in the mud. They had to pull me out or I would've died." With a quick bob of her head, she sat back in her chair. "Since then, I've had a crooked back. My clothes hang funny because the one side sticks out."

She swiveled around and pointed to the bulge on the right side of her back. I stared, thinking my back was sort of like hers.

"I have to go to work and fix all my clothes, so they hang straight," Grandma said.

I smiled hearing Grandma's favorite expression—"go to work." Whenever she explained how to do something, she prefaced the instructions with, "You go to work and . . ."

"I think you ought to take her to the chiropractor," Grandma said to Mom.

"Chiropractor?" I asked.

Grandma waved a hand. "For an adjustment."

"She's not going to any chiropractor." Mom tossed her tape measure on the table.

"What about that bone doctor?" Grandma asked.

"I'll think about it. Maybe talk to Millie," Mom said.

My Aunt Millie lived on the other side of the swimming pool, and she was a nurse. I thought she worked on the women's surgery floor. Would she know anything about legs?

When school started, thoughts of my lopsidedness receded. I had just celebrated my birthday—the big sixteen—but I had to wait until I finished drivers' education to take the test for my license. My junior year schedule included band again, and Gina and I were assigned to the same German and algebra classes. We had the misfortunate of getting Zylphia, the renowned cheerleading coach, as our algebra teacher.

Dad warned me about Zylphia. "She's a tough bird," he said. "I had her for one of my math classes." But he revealed no more about the woman with the strange name.

How tough could this woman be? She must be close to retirement age by now. Yet everyone feared her. I only took junior algebra because Gina insisted. An excellent math student, she liked nothing better than the challenge of a tough equation.

The first day of algebra class, my underarms dripped, my heart galloped, and my stomach clenched when I entered the classroom. I gathered strength from Gina, sitting next to me, looking as relaxed as ironed hair. I didn't wait long before the notorious teacher breezed into the room on her stiletto heels. She was short but substantial. A stack of bootblack hair, gleaming as if it had been spit-shined, framed her chiseled face. Her bulging eyes scrutinized the class as if looking for cooties, then she called out the roll, posed next to her desk, her hefty bosom heaving against her snug red suit. When she came to my name, she paused a second. "Did I teach your brother, Darwin, and . . . your sister, Jo?" she asked me.

99

Unable to believe her excellent memory, I said, "They are my cousins from different families." I thought it best not to mention she also taught my father.

"They were excellent students." She lifted her chin. Her glare challenged me to be as brilliant as my cousins, but I doubted that would happen.

I smiled into her coal black eyes, her lashes so heavily coated with mascara they resembled sweeper brushes. When she finished her silent assessment of me and moved on to intimidate the next student, I settled four inches lower in my desk and dreaded the long year ahead.

For the first time in many years, Zylphia wasn't directing the Junior Jam. I counted my blessings. Auditions were held in the auditorium, one of the original school structures. Plenty of students filled the worn wooden seats, hoping for a role or a bit part. The director adjusted his horn-rimmed glasses, smoothed his bushy mustache, and set to work casting for the musical comedy, "Sink or Swim." The story was set in 1888 aboard a showboat, which was suffering a decline in business because of mediocre show performances. In an effort to save the boat, the owner was auditioning new acts.

"You," the director pointed to me, "with the big mouth, you get a line. Say, 'But all the good talent went upstream with the first class boats,'" he ordered.

I don't know where he got the impression I had a big mouth, but I was thrilled to have a line. With authority, I delivered the line.

"Good," he said.

"Thanks, but I was hoping to be considered for one of the acts that audition for the showboat. I play the guitar and sing."

He put one hand on his hip. "And what, pray tell, would you like to sing?"

"What would you like me to sing?"

He snorted and threw up his hands. "Let me think about it."

"Thanks. I can bring my guitar to the next rehearsal."

"Sure, sure."

My year of guitar lessons and two years of self-instruction paid off. I got the director's okay to sing and play "The Cruel War." The "act" included my friend Nell, her friend Helen, and two boys. The musical earned rave reviews despite the incongruity of my playing an electric guitar while dressed in period 1880s clothes.

Being part of the Junior Jam, however, didn't earn me favors from Zylphia, who seemed to harbor resentment because she wasn't directing. She also disapproved of the pom-poms the Flag and Shield Girls incorporated into the half-time performances because she claimed we were trying to be cheerleaders.

For years Zylphia coached varsity cheerleaders like a drill sergeant. The football coach was a cupcake compared to Zylphia, but her methods of discipline proved rewarding—trophies for the best squad in the state year after year. At football games, Zylphia planted herself next to her husband in the front row on the fifty-yard line. Bundled inside her coat, her muffler hiding her sagging chin, Zylphia yelled commands to her squad while her husband sat stone-faced by her side.

Monday morning math class began with a critique of the weekend game. After a warm-up lap around her desk, she attacked the cheerleaders, the players, and the attendees of the game. Her purple heels clicked over the pockmarked wooden floor, and, as if she were searching for her whistle, she instead smoothed the front of her violet jacket before beginning her review.

"Kathy," Zylphia snapped, "your back flips lacked polish Friday night. Do you think we could see some improvement by the next game?"

"Yes ma'am," Kathy said without her usual peppy spirit.

"And while you're practicing, don't forget to point your toes at the end of the routine. You looked as if you were wearing cowboy boots."

Zylphia continued pacing the front of the room. She rarely sat at the desk.

"Mac, what was wrong with you?" she asked the football player.

Slouching in his chair, Mac grinned. "What?"

"You ran slower than a snail when you managed to catch a pass," Zylphia said.

Mac shrugged, still grinning.

"Sit up when I speak to you," Zylphia barked.

As if he'd been shocked by a cattle prod, Mac jerked upright and tucked his long legs under the small desk.

"Well, I hope you practice harder this week so you won't embarrass yourself . . . or the team. How do you expect to win a championship?" Zylphia scolded him, and then with lips pressed tightly together, she surveyed the room of cowering students, seeking her next victim.

Zylphia looked at me with what I thought might be a smile—lips peeled back exposing horse teeth—but it mutated into a sneer. I broke into a sweat.

"How much of the football game did you see, Debbie?" She said my name as if it left a bad taste on her tongue.

"Some," I said, my mouth as dry as dirt.

"I don't see how you watched any of the game because you were walking back and forth in front of me. Back and forth," she said, striding before her desk to imitate my perceived behavior. "Back and forth. It seems you girls are more interested in drawing attention to yourselves than in sitting in the stands and watching the game. I saw you pass in front of me at least a half dozen times." She stopped walking and scowled at me.

"I'm afraid that wasn't me you saw," I blurted out. "I was in the marching band, so I did parade up and down the football field." I heard Mac snicker. "After half-time, I changed clothes and sat in the stands for the fourth quarter."

Refusing to admit she had confused me with someone else, Zylphia countered. "That's what makes it so remarkable, that you could do all that walking in front of me in so short a time." She huffed a bit more and finally turned her attention to math.

Throughout the country, hippies cried for peace and love, but there was neither peace nor love doled out in algebra class. Every day I wanted to quit, not because of the work but because of the humiliation. But Gina, the star student, urged me on.

*　　*　　*

# CHAPTER FOURTEEN—BAD NEWS

I sat next to Mom in a narrow room filled with broken people. While Mom tended to paperwork, I looked around and worried. A teenager in a leg cast, a woman in a knee brace, a middle-age man with crutches, and an elderly woman in an arm sling stared at the morning show on the television and waited.

Mom had talked to my Aunt Millie who suggested I see the doctor for my lopsidedness. "I noticed Debbie's unusual walk at the swimming pool," my aunt had told Mom. Concerned, Mom had immediately called an orthopedic surgeon and scheduled me an appointment for mid October.

I couldn't imagine what the doctor would do to me. Grandma told me he would probably just take x-rays. X-rays! When I was in sixth grade, I had a physical for Girl Scout camp where a routine x-ray showed a kidney abnormality. I was hospitalized and underwent a procedure, which turned up nothing, so the doctors concluded the x-ray film must have been defective. I decided I didn't care much for doctors or hospitals, and I didn't exactly trust x-rays.

An unmarked door in the waiting room opened, and a lady in a white uniform said, "Debbie, you may come in now."

Mom followed me to a small room that smelled like the inside of a hospital.

The lady handed me a gown. "Take everything off except your panties and put this on. The doctor will be in shortly."

I didn't wait long before Dr. Haydon, a short man with thinning hair, entered the room. His red bow tie beamed above the lapels of his white lab coat. "Well, how are we today?" he asked as he sat on a stool with wheels.

"Fine," Mom spoke up. "I don't know if you remember me, but I think I went to school with you." She told him her maiden name.

Inwardly I groaned. Wherever we went, Mom or Dad always knew someone.

He peered at her through his thick glasses. "Yes, I remember."

"We're here to see you because my daughter Debbie seems to be a little uneven." Mom explained the skirt problem while I squirmed on the examination table.

"Uneven. Well, let's take a look." He rose, rooted in his pocket, and pulled out a funny-looking hammer. He smiled at me. "We'll start with the easy stuff." He flipped the gown back to expose my legs and whacked me with his odd hammer, first on one knee, then the other. Each leg shot forward as if it had been shocked by an electrical current. Then he tapped on my ankles and even my elbows. "Would you stand up, please?" He motioned to the floor.

I stepped down on the little step jutting from the table bottom and onto the floor. He asked me to bend over and touch my toes. Never very flexible, I did the best I could as my gown swung loose and gaped open in the back. While I reached for my toes, the doctor pressed his hands over my back and hips as if he were checking me for ripeness. I prayed he wouldn't get a peek at my front side. After I walked, tiptoed, raised arms and legs like a puppet, and showed the doctor the dent in my right leg, he told me to get back on the table.

"Lie down," he said, moving to stand alongside.

He raised the gown above my waist and pushed on my hipbones. Next, he grabbed a tape and measured not only my leg lengths but also their circumferences. Then, he loosened a large safety pin from his coat pocket. "Oh, no," I thought. He had me close my eyes and tell him which leg he touched and whether the sensation was sharp or dull. Luckily, the exam wasn't painful.

"Good," he proclaimed when he had finished. "Let's get some pictures and see where we go from there." He opened the door and stepped out. "Betty, I want . . ."

After my x-rays, the doctor returned with an extra large envelope and sat at the small desk in the corner. "It's as you suspected," he began. "Debbie's left leg is about an inch and three quarters longer than her right."

Mom frowned and, for once, said nothing.

"That's a big difference," the doctor said. "It's caused her spine to curve." He plucked one x-ray film from the envelope and jabbed it under the metal clips of an illuminated white box that hung on the wall above the desk. He pointed to the shadowy picture. "Here you can see the curve in her spine. About eighteen degrees, I would guess. A lateral curve like this is called scoliosis." He looked up at Mom.

I hoped Mom understood what he was talking about because I was still trying to comprehend my inch and three quarters difference.

"What do you do for that?" Mom found her voice.

"Surgery to correct scoliosis is an extremely complex procedure and not indicated at this time. A person can live with an eighteen degree curve, but if Debbie continues her uneven gait, her curve will only get worse."

I thought of Grandma's crooked back.

"Our goal is to even up her legs. It looks as if that muscle in her right leg didn't develop properly, stunting the growth in that leg. If Debbie were still growing, we could have slowed the growth in the bigger leg. But the x-rays show she is fully-grown—five foot, four inches."

"What do you propose, then?" Mom asked.

The doctor corrected his posture and inhaled deeply. "In California, doctors have had good success shortening femurs of very tall girls as well as others who had leg-length discrepancies." He patted his thighs to show us where the femur was located.

I picked at my gown as the doctor continued. "If we shorten her longer leg, the curvature of her spine will not get any worse."

"Surgery?" Mom gasped and looked at me.

"I think that's the best solution," Dr. Haydon said.

I started to worry. What was going to happen to me? Wasn't surgery painful? I remembered my broken collar bone in sixth grade, the pain it caused.

"Now, let me get this straight. You don't fix the back, but you fix the leg?" Mom asked.

"That's right."

"I can't have surgery now," I said. "I'm in school."

"I realize that, and while you decide whether or not to go ahead with the surgery, I want you to wear a built-up shoe," the doctor said.

"What's that?" I asked.

Dr. Haydon spread his fingers about two inches apart. "We add height to your right shoe to even you out by giving you a bigger heel. Okay with you?" He looked at Mom for approval, and she nodded.

Dr. Haydon slapped the desk and rose. "Okay then. I want to get some more x-rays, but, this time, I want you to stand your right foot on some boards."

While I stood in front of the x-ray machine, the doctor slipped slivers of boards under my right foot until he was finally satisfied with the appropriate height. After he reviewed the latest x-rays, he scribbled a prescription for the shoe man who would alter two pairs of my shoes.

As the doctor handed the prescription to Mom, he said, "Do think seriously about the surgery."

"What exactly would you do?" she asked.

"We would remove an inch and a half of Debbie's femur, allowing for a quarter inch reduction during healing, and we'd insert a rod down the middle of the bone. She wouldn't need a cast because the sooner she begins weight-bearing, the sooner the two ends of the bone come together and form new bone."

The doctor drew a picture to demonstrate what the bone would look like after surgery and during healing. It looked like two pipes positioned end to end except for a two-inch gap between them. He drew arcs like bridges connecting the gaps, demonstrating where the new bone would form. Finally, the two ends would come together, and the arcs would smooth over.

"I see." Mom sat, thinking. "How long does that take— for the bones to heal?"

"Several months," he said.

My mouth dropped opened.

He looked at me. "You'll be on crutches for a while, I'm afraid."

"But, no cast?" Mom asked.

"No."

"What about swimming?" I asked.

"Once your stitches are removed, you can get in a pool but no vigorous activity."

*There goes my job and my spending money . . . and right before senior year.*

"It won't hurt to delay the surgery?" Mom asked.

"Not as long as she wears the built-up shoe."

When Mom ran out of questions for the doctor, we were dismissed for a couple months. On the silent trip home, I thought about my rotten luck. My birthmark drew plenty of attention, but now I would have to wear a weird shoe. I was turning into a freak. I might as well join the circus.

Privately wallowing in self-pity, I feigned happiness at school. No sense in making my friends suffer. While I waited for my new shoes to be finished, I concentrated on my studies. After enduring the rigorous rehearsal schedule for the Junior Jam, I thought I would have a bit of a break from my extracurricular activities. However, the marching band was invited to march in the homecoming parade at Illinois State University. Russ beamed with pride over the invitation, and he worked us hard to polish our parade performance.

On a crisp early morning, two buses, loaded with band members and chaperones, left the school and headed north. Arriving in Normal, Illinois, after a three-and-a-half hour trip, we changed into our uniforms. By parade time, a blustery wind sent currents of icy air against the bare skin below my shorts. Goosebumps rose and I shivered despite the extra layers beneath my sweater. When we started marching, I thought I would warm up, but the wind intensified and chilled every inch of me. I expected the shield girls to sail away still clinging to their flimsy letters.

Just as we approached the judge's platform, a ferocious gust ripped my tam off the top of my head. It dangled by a bobby pin in my hair. I grabbed at the tam while trying to control the pole, its flag buffeted by the winds. The wind tangled my hair around the lone bobby pin, and I couldn't loosen it. I saw the judges' platform ahead, and with one last frantic attempt, I yanked the tam from the side of my head. I stuffed the tam, laden with strands of hair and loose bobby pins, into my right hand that held the flagpole. Just in time— eyes right. I turned my head and smiled at the judges, hoping they didn't notice my missing headgear.

I was never so happy to complete a parade. Like human Popsicles, the band melted back into the buses for the long ride home. Bobby, the red-haired trumpet player, finagled his way on the bus with the Flag and Shield Girls. He made the rounds teasing, flirting, and begging. No one took him seriously. His tales were taller than he was.

I happened to be sitting on the armrest of the bus seat, my feet in the aisle, talking with the girls across the aisle when Bobby sauntered up to me. He slung his arm around me as if we were best buddies. "What are you doing, beautiful?" With his face so close to mine, I could count his freckles.

I moved my head back. "Talking. What do you want?"

He moved closer, his brown eyes shining. "Baby, I need a kiss."

I leaned back a little more. "Get out of here."

Bobby laughed and then put his free hand over his heart. "Oh, the coldness of a woman. You're breaking my heart."

He reminded me of Eddie Haskell, the scheming, obnoxious friend of Wally on "Leave it to Beaver," such a wise guy. "Bobby, go back to your seat."

He grasped my hand. "You are so beautiful—your hair, your eyes, your body. Come on, babe. Just one kiss."

I disentangled myself from his soft hand with its long, slender fingers and chuckled. "No. Go away." Bobby talked that way to every girl. I had overheard it before. He was on a constant quest to find a girl who would like him. Although I did like him for some strange reason, perhaps because he was so persistent, I had dismissed his advances.

Suddenly, Bobby lunged forward and planted a kiss square on my mouth. His momentum pushed me over, and I fell backwards into the seat. I thrashed beneath the weight of his body. "Get off me!" I pushed hard against him and wriggled into a sitting position. "Don't ever do that."

"Oh, baby, I'll remember this moment forever," he said as he sat up.

I gave him a shove. "You're crazy. Now, get out of here."

As he sauntered up the aisle, I groaned and tried to hide my grin. When would that boy give up?

\*     \*     \*

## CHAPTER FIFTEEN—SHOE TROUBLES

When Mom presented me with my two altered right shoes she had retrieved from the shoemaker, I wanted to quit school. The shoes were ugly. Although constructed to blend with the shoe, the heel reminded me of the chunks of 2x4s that Grandpa strapped to my tricycle pedals when I was a child. The new height modification should have made me straighter, but I felt like a listing ship. My shoe collection had always been meager because of my narrow feet, but now my choices were limited to the revised saddle oxfords or loafers. No tennis shoes, no heels, no sandals . . . not even a different pair of loafers. But I needed to wear my tennis shoes for band to finish out the season. After the Hobo Day parade, the Thanksgiving Day football game, and the Santa Claus parade, I would have to retire my tennis shoes.

Since Mom wouldn't hear of me quitting school, and Zylphia certainly wouldn't approve even one absence from algebra class, I laced up my oxfords, threw on my life preserver, and sailed to school.

During band practice, I couldn't heft the new shoe as easily as the other. Russ noticed my unwieldy right shoe while I was rehearsing kick steps. He frowned. "Having trouble?"

"Yes," I said. "I found out I'm a little uneven, so I have to wear a built-up shoe."

My band instructor shook his head of red hair and grinned. "Well, I always thought you marched fine with one foot on the curb."

I laughed and nodded in agreement. "Naturally talented, I guess."

He gave me a soft pat on the shoulder. "Do the best you can."

In my mind, my shoe stood out like a red pimple, yet few people noticed it, except for Mac, the football jock who sat next to me in algebra class. "Cool shoes," he said when he caught a glimpse of my fat-heeled shoe. He couldn't see the normal shoe, so he didn't notice the two were different. Eventually, I accepted my new shoe and adjusted to the gait.

Hobo Day was fast approaching, and I worked on the class float as often as possible. Construction took place at the Crest Mountain Fire Department, which made it very convenient for the Crest Mountain crowd. Naturally, Brian made regular appearances, his magnetism never failing to attract me. Often times Bobby showed up even though he wasn't in my class. He talked big around the guys and tried to charm the girls. Now and then I'd catch him gazing at me. When our eyes met, he winked as if he knew a secret.

A rainy, November Hobo Day neither hampered the festivities nor drowned the floats. Wearing hobo clothes like the rest of the students, the band splashed down Main Street, leading the parade. At the courthouse, the cheerleaders, dry and peppy, emerged from their closed convertible cocoons to lead the rally.

Surrounded by football players, the dean complimented the team on a winning season thus far—no losses and one tie. "Tomorrow we will conquer the East Side Flyers." He concluded his speech as the crowd screamed for the coveted conference trophy. He signaled for quiet. "Now, the winner of the best float is . . . the juniors . . . class of 1969." I couldn't believe my class won! We had come a long way since that disastrous freshman float.

The next day, Thanksgiving, the rain had stopped, but yesterday's deluge had left the football field as boggy as a swamp. By halftime, like tractors, the players had ploughed furrows in the field. I lined up with the band, ready for the season's final performance. I took my first steps onto the field, and my gleaming white tennis shoes squished into the muddy grass. "These are ruined," I thought. Counting off ten steps per every five-yard line, I concentrated on my routine as I moved downfield. On my heels, the band sounded exceptionally strong.

Marching became a struggle—me against the mud. With each step, my foot sank into the muck. Mud splashed my socks and legs. I saw the other girls battling the uneven, mushy terrain. Towards the middle of the field, the ground got even worse. The deeper I sank, the more difficulty I had pulling my feet from the muddy bog. I wondered how the tuba player was faring.

All of a sudden, the mud swallowed my right shoe like a hungry animal. I paused a split second, my white sock poised above the ground to take the next step, my brain deciding what to do. With the musicians following me, I couldn't stop to pull my shoe from its grave, so I placed my stocking foot on the wet turf and kept going.

Just when I feared I'd lose my sock, too, the Flag and Shield Girls neared the sidelines for the conclusion of the performance. When the girls noticed I had lost my shoe, they chuckled softly. I just kept smiling. In front of the cheerleaders, the girls and I danced our pom-pom routine with high-kicks. When the mud from our shoes sailed toward the cheerleaders, they squealed and hurried their pretty uniforms back a few steps. From her perch, Zylphia glowered. The thought of Monday's algebra class gave me a shiver—or maybe my foot was half frozen.

The final notes faded, and the band filed off the field. Someone passed me my muddy shoe as I hobbled toward the band room to rinse my legs and feet, change my clothes, and slip on my built-up shoe. I wanted a soak in a hot tub, but I had to see the end of the game. The mud-bath on the field continued, and when the final buzzer sounded, the Maroons had lost the battle to their rivals. But the war was ongoing, and who knew what would happen next year?

The following day, I hung up my tennis shoes after marching in the Santa Claus parade. I didn't know it at the time, but my marching days were over.

X-rays taken at Dr. Haydon's office in mid December revealed no radical changes in my curved spine. "How are you doing with your built-up shoe?" The doctor asked me.

I wanted to tell him I hated it because it was heavy and awkward, but I said, "Fine."

"Good. Keep wearing it." He turned his attention to Mom. "Have you given any thought to the surgery?"

"Yes, we've discussed it, and Debbie wants to have the surgery."

"You realize the alternative is to wear the built-up shoe?"

Mom nodded. "Yes."

The doctor looked at me. "So, you prefer to have the operation?"

"Yes. I can't wear a shoe like this for the rest of my life."

"I understand." Dr. Haydon scribbled something on my record. "I suggest we get you on the surgery schedule as soon as school ends. That will give me time to do my homework on the procedure."

Mom folded her arms across her chest. "Excuse me? You've never performed this procedure before?"

"No, not to correct a leg-length discrepancy."

She cleared her throat. "But you have *some* experience?"

"Please be assured I have performed countless intramedullary fixations for fractures."

His big words must have convinced Mom he knew what he was doing because she unfolded her arms and nodded. The doctor wanted to see me again in two months; meanwhile, I had to wear my shoe.

Winter, seemingly unending, dulled my spirit. My girlfriends were already thinking ahead to college. I couldn't think beyond my next doctor visit. Many of my friends wanted to be teachers, but having taught swimming lessons, I wasn't all that keen to make teaching my life profession. After my guidance counselor reviewed my aptitude tests, he determined I was best suited for secretarial work. I laughed because I couldn't type or take shorthand, and I had never taken any business courses. The high school classes I had been taking were geared to fulfill college entrance requirements. I figured I'd be going to college, but where and for what I didn't know.

While I marked time waiting for my surgery, I concentrated on my studies. I suffered through algebra, German, and physics; however, I enjoyed my stimulating English class. Always a voracious reader, I discovered writing tweaked my interest, too. The teacher encouraged the class to write in a journal, and she praised my abilities.

By spring, my girlfriends and I had finished ogling basketball players and turned our attention to the track team. A hurdler named Randy caught my eye. The husky, muscled boy flew over hurdles like a roadrunner. He ran just as fast away from me.

At the meets, the girls and I met three guys, former track athletes, who had graduated the previous year. To avoid the draft and stay out of Vietnam, they attended the local junior college. Before long, Gabe and I started seeing one another. I honestly don't know why I dated him. I wasn't attracted to him the same way I had been to Brian or even Alex, and he wasn't the most interesting date because all he talked about was running. But he did invite my friends and me to college dances, and he did have a car, even though it was a hand-painted, grass green, 1948 Chevy with one functioning door.

Throughout the spring, my girlfriends and I chased the runners, caught a couple, traded boyfriends, and had some laughs. No one got too serious with the changing arrangements. Gina, who shed her braces, kept us guessing whether her romance with Mark was on or off.

To celebrate the school year's conclusion (and my final B in algebra), I hosted a swim party, my last hurrah before my surgery. I had never considered myself popular, well-known maybe, but I didn't hang out with the cheerleaders or the student council members. Yet word of my party had spread through school faster than a sprinter's best time.

The night of the party, I went from worrying that no one would come to managing a mob. Cars clogged my street as well as the vacant field behind the pool house. Kids roamed my back yard, the fields, and the streets. I never saw Brian among the partiers, although Bobby and the Crest Mountain crowd had made an appearance. Most of the boys swam while the girls strutted the deck, refusing to get in the water and ruin their hairdos. As the night wore on, the music got louder, the kids more rambunctious. Boys rode skateboards off the diving board and tossed fully-clothed girls into the water. Luckily, no one was injured. They seemed to be having fun, and the boys who had ignored me in grade school complimented me on a great party. Long after midnight, the crowd departed, leaving in its wake a path of destruction equal to a small hurricane.

I awoke the next morning and went to the pool house before breakfast. Mom already had her broom in motion. "I can't believe this mess," she said as she swept up a pile of debris.

"Sorry, Mom." I yawned. "It was a great party. Thanks." I kissed her on the cheek. "I'll clean this up."

"No, that's all right. Go have some breakfast." She shooed me toward the door with the broom. "Make sure your brother and sister get fed," she added.

Later that day I went to school to pick up my yearbook as the final act of my junior year. Students meandered the campus, swapping books to record messages of inspiration, amusement, or embarrassment. My friend Jane wrote in my book, "Maybe some great changes will come this summer." I didn't know how true those words would be.

\*　　　\*　　　\*

# Transitions

## CHAPTER SIXTEEN—CUT IT OUT

On my big day, June 19, 1968, I fidgeted between the starched sheets of my hospital bed. I didn't know what to expect after my surgery, but from the expressions on my parents' faces, I knew I wasn't in for a relaxing vacation. Dad paced the confines of my semi-private room while Mom sat in a chair that was crammed in the corner near the window. For the umpteenth time, I smoothed the thin, yellow blanket that covered me. The rough gown I wore glided effortlessly over my prepped and shaved left leg as I wiggled beneath the bedding.

Mom glanced at the empty bed next to me. "Looks like you're here by yourself."

Just then Dr. Haydon breezed into the room, dressed in green scrubs. I barely recognized him without his trademark bowtie. "Good morning," he said and whipped back the covers to expose my suntanned legs. "Now, which leg are we working on?"

Once I was settled, the man maneuvered the gurney into the hall. "Tell your folks good-bye."

With eyes glistening, Mom leaned over me and gave me a hug and kiss. "We'll be right here when you get back."

Then Dad brushed a light kiss on my forehead and patted my arm. "See you soon."

"Bye," I mouthed and fluttered a hand.

Without my contact lenses or glasses, I couldn't make out much on my trip to the operating room. I shivered under a mound of blankets. The gurney sped through the corridors, and I was mesmerized by the ceiling tiles flying over my head. An automatic door whooshed open, and the gurney bumped over the threshold into another world. Green-clad, fuzzy figures bustled past me. The porter whisked me into a room, docked my chariot in line with others, and wished me luck. I squinted at the blurry lumps on the stretchers around me, but I felt very alone.

Suddenly, a man in a fitted green cap loomed above me. "I'm the anesthesiologist." He read my patient armband. "Who's your doctor, and what's he going to do?"

My heart pounded. If he didn't know what was happening, I could be in trouble. I mumbled a response that sounded like baby talk.

"Good, just checking. I need to start an IV on you . . . to give you some fluids."

I smiled, vaguely remembering the instructions about the surgery. After another needle assault, I was moved to the operating room and transferred onto the table. Masked, gowned figures scurried about performing their tasks. The last thing I remembered was the muffled laughter when the nurses uncovered my legs and read my message.

*     *     *

In a haze of discomfort, I awakened to find Mom at my bedside. "Hi, sweetheart," she said, caressing my face. "You're back in your room."

"Good," I whispered.

"The doctor said everything went fine. Would you like some ice chips?"

I nodded and accepted the moisture. "Where's Dad?"

"He just stepped out. How do you feel?"

I tried to look at my leg, but I was flat on my back. "I'm not sure." My eyes heavy, I fell back asleep.

Sometime later, pain roused me from my medicated state. "Oh," I groaned.

Mom stepped into my line of sight. "I'm here."

"My heel is on fire."

"Your heel is on fire?"

"Yes, I can't stand it." I moaned again, then gingerly touched my left thigh and found it heavily padded. I breathed a small sigh of relief, knowing the doctor shortened the correct leg, but why did my heel hurt? "Can you move it or something?"

"I better call the nurse."

After giving me an injection for the pain, the nurse checked my heel. "I think I can fix the problem." She disappeared.

The medication quickly soothed the throbbing in my left thigh, but the burn in my heel continued. Mom gently massaged it with lotion. "You're just not used to these rough sheets."

The nurse returned and placed a circular foam pad with a hole in its middle under my left ankle so the heel dangled off the sheet. "Feel better?" she asked.

"Yes, that helps. Thanks."

Mom smoothed back my long hair. "The doctor says you will be getting out of bed tomorrow."

I gave her a half smile. "That should be fun."

"Oh look, here comes your dinner."

The nurse set a tray on the over-bed table and elevated the head of the bed to a thirty-degree angle. Mom uncovered a bowl and declared, "Pea soup."

I nearly gagged. "Ehew! I hate pea soup. Get that smelly stuff away from me."

"Umm, how about some Jell-O?"

"I'm not hungry."

She waved a spoonful of lime gelatin in front of me. "Why don't you try a few bites?"

"Is everything around here green?"

"Come on, be a good girl."

I managed to get down some of the liquid fare. Dad arrived as Mom was tidying my table. "How's the patient?" he asked.

"I'm okay, just hurting."

"You know what Dad said to me as you were being wheeled away?" Mom asked. "He said, 'I wonder if she'll change her mind.'"

"I'm glad it's over," I said.

Tight-lipped, Dad gazed down at me. "You're braver than me."

I looked at them and did my best to smile, and then I noticed the flowers sitting on the window sill. "Who are those from?"

"Dad and me." Mom picked them up and brought them closer for me to see.

I sniffed the carnation arrangement that looked like an ice cream soda. "Thanks. They're beautiful."

Mom and Dad hovered near, as if wanting to absorb my pain. But eventually they had to leave to check on Roger and Diane, who were in Grandma's care. Throughout the night, the nurses observed my dressing and drain, changed my IVs, checked my circulation, and made certain I was comfortable.

Before breakfast, Dr. Haydon showed up, dressed in a suit and his usual bow tie. A nurse with a chart followed behind. The chipper doctor asked, "Well, how are we today?"

I had barely opened my eyes. "You tell me."

He uncovered my left leg. "Let's take a look." He examined the dressing and drain, then my leg. "Wiggle your toes."

Although I obeyed, the simple task hurt.

The doctor pointed to the side of my leg and told the nurse, "I don't like how her leg is externally rotated. Put a pillow here to keep it in alignment. Not much drainage in the Hemovac?"

"No, sir," the nurse said.

Dr. Haydon fired off orders that sounded like Greek to me. "Have her fitted for crutches, and have her stand at the bedside today—no weight bearing on the left leg," he finished telling the nurse. "Debbie, everything is going fine. We'll get you standing today, and tomorrow you can begin crutch training in physical therapy. Is that okay with you?"

"I guess so."

"If you need anything, let the nurse know." He hustled on his way.

Breakfast and Mom showed up at the same time. From a more upright position, I assessed my food, the smells tempting me. While Mom opened my milk, she rattled off the names of everyone who had called to inquire about me.

I balanced a spoonful of eggs toward my mouth. "Did you talk to Gina?"

"Of course. She said she'd come to see you tomorrow."

"That's good." I pointed to my food. "This isn't too bad."

"Drink your milk."

I took a swallow of the tepid milk. "The doctor was already here."

"What did he say?"

"I get to stand at the bedside today and start crutch walking tomorrow."

Mom smiled. "That's good."

After breakfast, a nurse around Mom's age breezed in the room.

"Hi, Shirley," Mom said.

"Well, hello, Mae. I saw the last name, but I didn't know this was your daughter."

Mom introduced the nurse who was married to one of Dad's bowling buddies.

"I have three pills for you—a vitamin, an antibiotic, and something to keep things working properly." She winked at Mom. "Are you ready to get out of bed?" she asked me.

"I guess so."

"Good. I'll send in a couple nurses to help you."

It took two young nurses to maneuver me and my leg to the edge of the bed, one agonizing inch at a time. Mom watched the proceedings from the foot of my bed. One of my helpers slowly pivoted my left leg off the bed, supporting it as it jutted out above the floor.

The other helper cozied up to my side and wrapped an arm around my back. "Good. Now put your arm around my shoulders. As you stand up, the leg goes down, but don't put any weight on it. Understand?"

I suddenly felt warm all over. "Yes."

"Are you ready?"

"Let's go."

With one arm around the nurse, I pushed myself off the bed with my free hand, my right foot searching for the floor. The nurse who held my left leg as straight as a stick eased it to a normal vertical position. All of my one hundred and five pounds weighed upon my left leg like a bowling ball balanced on a paper straw. Sweat dampened my forehead, and I held my breath against the pain. I looked down at my left leg, the leg missing an inch and a half of bone. I expected to see it detach.

"Don't look down," the nurse ordered. "Chin up and breathe."

I raised my head and sucked in some air, then noticed I could see out my window. I saw the walkway leading to the front entrance of the hospital and envied the two-legged pedestrians. My dented right leg quivered.

"Okay, that's enough," the nurse said. "Back in bed, fanny first, then the leg."

Once I was settled in bed, I inhaled deeply and expelled a long breath. Standing up was harder than I thought it would be. I surrendered to the effects of a pain pill and dozed until Mom woke me for lunch. While I was eating, a lady wearing the pink apron of a volunteer entered with a vase of red roses. She smiled broadly, verified my name, and then placed the bouquet next to my lunch tray.

"Aren't those beautiful?" Mom took a whiff of the flowers.

"I'll say. I wonder who sent them." I stared up at the tall flowers.

Mom plucked the note from the arrangement and handed it to me. "Read the card."

I opened the tiny envelope and silently scanned the brief message. I sighed and read aloud, "Debbie, get well soon. The roses mean I love you. Bobby." With a moan, I tossed the card on the table.

"Isn't that nice?"

I shook my head and frowned.

*       *       *

# CHAPTER SEVENTEEN—MY FELLOW SUFFERER

Cruising on the effects of my last pain pill, I stared at a television program while I munched on the popcorn Mom had left me. Through the doorway, arm in arm, walked a man and a woman led by a hospital employee.

"You have a new roommate," the clerk announced. "This is Mrs. . . ."

"Jo. Please, call me Jo," the woman interrupted.

I swallowed my mouthful of popcorn. "Hi. I'm Debbie."

The blond woman's broad smile overshadowed her rounded body. "Nice to meet you." She stood awkwardly next to the neatly made-up bed. "When did you have surgery?"

"Yesterday."

The woman giggled like a ten-year-old. "Yesterday! And you are already eating popcorn?"

"Yes, I was dying for something salty."

She laid a hand on the man next to her. "I'm sorry. This is my husband, Kenny."

A balding man as large as a linebacker hustled around the empty bed and extended a hand the size of a football. "Howdy," he said in a strong voice.

I grasped the monstrous hand. "Hello."

He smiled at me, and wrinkles formed at the corners of his brown eyes. He released my hand and returned to his wife's side.

Jo began to place her belongings in drawers. "I hope I look as chipper as you after my surgery tomorrow. What kind of surgery did you have?"

"Orthopedic. They shortened one of my legs."

Jo's cornflower blue eyes widened. "Wow! You look great."

"Thanks. But you should have seen me this morning hanging on two nurses who were helping me stand up. Not a pretty picture. Tomorrow I start physical therapy."

She sat down on her bed. "I'm sure you'll do fine."

A nurse entered and drew the privacy curtain. I heard her say she had some questions and instructions for my new roommate. I went back to watching TV and tried to ignore the interview. Although Jo was around my mom's age, I was grateful for the company. None of my friends had visited yet.

And now that my surgery was over, Mom couldn't sit with me all day. She had Roger and Diane to think about, too. If I knew my brother, he was tired of Grandma by now. And Grandma was probably worn out by my almost four-year-old sister. I hated to admit I missed my brother and sister, but I did.

I glanced longingly out the window. The vase of roses sitting on the sill caught my attention, and I was reminded of Bobby. He couldn't have meant that he loved me. Could he? Sure, he was always hanging around my friends and me, but he was like a little brother—underfoot and irritating. Still I tolerated and accepted him as a friend, not a boyfriend. I didn't know what to say to him about his message. I was sure he would call or visit because he intruded on every event, with or without an invitation.

The nurse opened the curtain and left the room. My new roommate was tucked into bed, her husband parked in a chair next to her, holding her hand. He told her he had to leave and that he loved her, and then they kissed a long while before he left. Gosh! They acted like teenagers.

That evening Jo asked me about my family, school, and hobbies. Distracted by our conversation, I forgot the constant throbbing in my leg. "Do you have any children?" I asked.

She rolled onto her side to face me. "Yes, I have three sons—Richard, Jerry, and Lenny. Let's see, Richard's twenty-four, Jerry's twenty-one, and Lenny, the youngest, is twenty."

"Do they live around here?"

"No. Richard's stationed at Andrews Air Force Base in Maryland. He's married and has a little girl and a baby boy. Jerry's a banker and only been married a year. He and his wife live in Collinsville. And Lenny's in the army with the 101$^{st}$ Airborne. He's a Green Beret, home on leave from Vietnam."

When she spoke of her youngest son, her eyes twinkled and a smile tugged at her lips, making me think he was her favorite. "You must be glad he's home safe."

"I've been worried sick. I hadn't heard from him in weeks, so I called the Red Cross to explain I was having surgery and wanted to tell my son. The next thing I know Lenny's calling me from Hawaii to say he's on his way home—on emergency leave. He thought someone had died, but I told him I was just having surgery. The first thing he did when he got home was drive to McDonald's for a hamburger. Now he's off on a fishing trip with Jerry. But they'll be back this weekend." She smiled like a kid going to a birthday party.

"You and your husband must be very proud of your three sons."

"Actually, Kenny is the boys' stepfather. We've been married now for five years."

"He seems like a very nice man."

She nodded. "Oh, he's the best. I don't know what I'd do without him."

Before long it was bedtime. I never thought I could feel so exhausted by doing so little, but I dropped off to sleep in an instant.

Whispers roused me in the dark early morning hours—nurses preparing my roommate for surgery. My eyes fuzzy with sleep, I glimpsed a figure padding past my bed toward the bathroom. "Good morning," I mumbled.

The figure paused. "Oh, I'm so sorry to wake you."

I rubbed my face and stretched. "Time to get ready for your big day."

"Yes, so it seems. Please excuse me." Jo clutched the back of her hospital gown to cover herself and ducked into the bathroom."

When she emerged, she had removed yesterday's makeup and fluffed her hair. Her fair complexion brightened the shadowed room. "I feel *necked* without my makeup."

I thought of how I must look, even though I never wore too much makeup. "You look fine. Besides, you can put it on again after your surgery."

She slipped daintily into bed. "I just hate for anyone to see me."

"I guess the doctors and nurses are used to it."

Jo examined her fingers and let out a sigh. "I even had to remove my nail polish."

"Definitely unfair."

In the midst of Jo's pre-operative preparations, Dr. Haydon made his early appearance, accompanied by a nurse. He ripped at my bulky dressing like a child opening a Christmas present. While my skin tingled from the tape removal, he cut the suture that secured the drain and pulled out the long, plastic tube. My stomach rolled, and I turned my head.

The doctor inspected the incision. "Looks good." He faced the nurse. "Clean it up and cover the drain site with a 2x2."

"Should I also put a dressing over the incision?" she asked.

"Yes, you can put an 8x10 on it." The doctor then addressed me. "Today, you'll start physical therapy. Remember, don't put any weight on your left leg."

I nodded to him before he headed out the door, then peeked at my incision—a perfectly pink straight line, about six inches long, carved along the side of my leg midway between my knee and hip. Like ladder rungs, stiff black sutures anchored my skin together. I wondered how the doctor had fitted the rod into the middle of my bone. It must have been an engineering feat.

A short time later, while I tended to my bathing behind my curtained-off corner of the room, I yelled a farewell to my roommate as she left for surgery. After my bath, the nurses came in to begin the laborious process of getting me out of bed. At last, settled in a wheelchair, I was whisked away to the physical therapy department, my left leg pointing the way.

In a small room, crowded with exercise equipment, the therapist parked me between the parallel bars. She assisted me to a standing position and measured wooden crutches for the correct height while I gripped the bars and kept the weight off my left leg. The longer I stood between the bars, the heavier my leg felt. Pain flooded my thigh. My eyes watered and my arms shook as I tried to hold myself upright. The therapist noticed my discomfort and helped me back into the wheelchair. Even with my leg elevated again, the pain escalated.

"Take me back to my room," I cried.

After the therapist abandoned me in my room, my sobs poured forth. *I can't stand this.* The pain in my thigh gravitated to my hip as though the rod was trying to burrow out. I twisted in the chair, attempting to find a comfortable position, but my hip throbbed no matter which way I turned.

At last, a nurse arrived to find me sobbing. "I'll bring you a pain pill and then get you back in bed."

"No! No pain pill," I wailed. "I need a shot. I can't stand this. I think the rod is coming out my hip."

She frowned. "I'll call the doctor and be right back."

I tried to breathe slowly and pray, anything to distract myself from the torture. Seconds felt like hours. I clenched my fists and succumbed to tears. How can I bear this? Why must I suffer? My friends were all enjoying summer vacation while I fought to be normal.

Finally, the nurse returned and gave me an injection to ease the pain. As the medicine performed its magic, my sobs choked to a halt.

"The doctor wants to get an x-ray of your leg and hip— to check the position of the rod," the nurse said.

"I need to go to bed. I can't go to x-ray," I pleaded.

"No, we'll take a portable x-ray, so you won't have to leave the bed."

She helped into bed where I collapsed with exhaustion. At least the medicine was dulling the pain. I glared at the wheelchair folded in the corner and at my crutches propped alongside, and I wondered how I'd ever manage to walk again. I shouldn't have to go through this. It wasn't fair. Living with a birthmark was hard enough. If I had known the operation would have hurt this much, I might have reconsidered. My thoughts became foggy, and I drifted to sleep.

\*       \*       \*

I crashed into wakefulness, disturbed by a voice calling my name.

The x-ray technician shot a couple films of my leg and hurried on his way. The pain retreated as long as I didn't move my leg, so I basked in immobility until lunch. Revived by nourishment, I coasted through the afternoon.

According to the nurse, the x-rays turned out fine. The rod hadn't been displaced. In addition to that bit of good news, the nurse gave me a present—the piece of bone Dr. Haydon had removed from my leg. The inch-long specimen looked smaller in diameter than I had envisioned. On each end of the bone, two tiny notches, like pilot holes, had been bored out during the bone's removal. The outside of bone was as smooth as a hardwood floor; the inside was a rough, narrow tube. I remembered Dr. Haydon telling me my bone was so thick, he had to use the smallest rod manufactured to fit through its center. I guess I had only imagined the rod moving. Tomorrow I would get out of bed and learn to use my crutches and not worry about that rod.

More flowers arrived that afternoon—a mum arrangement from my girlfriends that looked like a puppy's face and an African violet plant from Bobby. This time the card read, "The violets mean I'll always be true." First roses, now violets. What next? That boy was crazy.

Suddenly, I heard someone moaning, and a gurney bearing my roommate glided into the room. Jo's moans became louder during her transfer into bed. When her husband was allowed in the room, he stroked her head and talked to her as if he were soothing a crying baby. After my ordeal, I knew how she felt.

Mom and Dad visited around dinnertime. I related the story of my pain-filled day and received their sympathy and encouragement. When Gina popped in for a visit, my parents departed, leaving us alone to catch up.

Gina cackled like a hen when she saw the flowers and read the cards from Bobby. "What are you going to do?"

"Do? I'm not going to do anything."

"Do you think he's serious?"

"Who knows? It's probably a joke."

Gina looked thoughtful. "Maybe."

For the remainder of visiting hours, Gina and I commiserated—her hot and cold romance with Mark, my painful recovery. Then she hugged me as best she could with me in bed and tiptoed out.

In the void, I wrestled with my loneliness. The soft snoring of my roommate was of little comfort to me.

*     *     *

# CHAPTER EIGHTEEN—THE SOLDIER

The following day wasn't as brutal as I had anticipated. Before I tackled crutch-walking, I downed a pain pill from the nurse. I waited in the wheelchair for the physical therapist and pictured my nerve endings swaddled in cotton, insulated against any painful stimuli. Instead of taking me on a long trip to the physical therapy department, the therapist wheeled me into the wide corridor outside my room and set the brakes on the chair. After fastening a wide belt around my waist, she assisted me to a standing position and handed me the crutches. "Crutches and operative leg first and then the other leg," she instructed.

Feeling secure with the therapist's hand gripping the belt, I moved the crutches and my left leg forward. I leaned into the step, putting weight on my hands while pushing off my right leg and then bringing the leg even with the crutches. Half expecting pain to cripple my progress, I steadied myself, surprised to discover just a mild heaviness in my left leg.

Behind me the therapist cheered. "Good! Now try another step."

I repeated the process. Although dizziness threatened, I inched ahead. "Hey, I'm walking!" After five measured steps, exhaustion descended like dense fog, and I swayed between the wooden sticks, my heart pounding.

"Okay, let's swivel around and go back to the chair," the therapist said.

When I turned around, the chair beckoned to me, but it looked as if it were a mile away. I inhaled deeply and plunged onward. Inch by inch I closed the gap. Finally, I reached the chair, feeling like pudding. The therapist poured me into the chair, elevated my left leg, and rolled me back to my room. Thankfully, neither my leg nor hip hurt like the previous day. I rested comfortably in the chair, pleased with my tiny accomplishment.

While I had been racing down the hall, my roommate had finished her bed bath and dabbed on some makeup. "You look nice," I said.

Jo groaned. "Thanks—just trying to look human."

I laughed. "I know how you feel. The first day is the hardest."

Mom came to visit after lunch. She gave Jo a Get Well card that had her laughing between her groans. The two women chatted while I went with the therapist for another trek down the hall. Later, I lounged in bed, my reward for a day of hard work.

Bobby finally telephoned and asked if I had received the flowers. I thanked him without commenting on his messages. I didn't want to encourage him.

Saturday mirrored the previous day—more crutch training. The nurses got Jo out of bed for the first time, and our recoveries seemed to be progressing on a slow schedule without complications.

Early Sunday morning Jo began primping for expected company—her sons. She bubbled with excitement as she applied her makeup, fixed her hair, and changed into a nightgown she had brought from home.

Feeling as if I had just finished a Hell Night sorority initiation, I decided to spruce up, too. I brushed my limp, dirty hair into two high pigtails and fastened on ribbons. Next, I swiped on face powder and a trace of blush. When I peered into the tiny mirror in the over-bed table, I had to grin. What did I expect? I was in bed, still wearing the standard hospital gown. I wished I could put on real clothes, wash my hair, and take a bath. With a sigh, I folded away the mirror.

Sometime after lunch, I heard a voice call, "Where's my mom?" and a tall man who looked as if he could use a few home-cooked meals marched into the room, followed by Jo's husband. Wearing a big smile, the newcomer leaned over Jo and gave her a kiss.

She giggled like a school girl and embraced him. "I've missed you. How was your fishing trip?"

The man untangled himself from her clutches and stood up. "Fine, but I landed a fish hook in my face." He pointed to a spot below his eye.

Jo motioned for him to come closer. "Let me see."

He bent down so she could inspect his injury. "I could've put my eye out."

Jo patted his cheek. "My poor baby."

The man with military-cut brown hair snapped upright again. He stepped back and glanced around the room while Kenny gave his wife a long kiss and then took a chair next to her. The newcomer's eyes, the color of a clear summer sky, skimmed past me.

Jo struggled to a more upright position. "Son, this is my roommate, Debbie." Jo raised a hand in my direction. "Debbie, this is my youngest son, Lenny."

When his eyes rested on me, I suddenly felt self-conscious, but I smiled. "Nice to meet you. I've heard a lot about you from your mom."

He wrinkled his broad forehead, drawing his thick brows together. "Whatever she told you is a lie."

"Oh, really?" I asked.

"I'm not even sure she's my mother. When I was young, she threatened to sell me to the gypsies." A smile formed on his thin lips. "What mother would do that?"

I watched his smile widen, exposing a gap between his front teeth. "She was probably trying to keep you under control."

Lenny chuckled and began to relate his fishing trip adventures. I watched his dramatic antics, which clearly entertained his mom and stepfather. I couldn't help remembering that Lenny had just returned from Vietnam.

How could a man who had recently experienced the savagery of war appear so happy and unaffected? Too self-absorbed, I rarely thought about the war, nor did I know anyone serving in the military, except for Mom's cousin whom I never met. I tried not to gawk at the lively group, but I was held prisoner by my bed, excluded from the intimacy of their family.

Lenny slid his hands into his pockets. "So, what are you in for?" he asked me.

I touched my left leg. "I had my leg shortened."

He winced. "That must have hurt."

"More than I thought it would. But it feels a little better each day."

"That's good. So, do you have any sisters?"

For a second, I didn't understand where his question was leading. Then I realized he might be searching for a date while he was home on leave. And he obviously thought I was too young and too crippled to consider. I smirked. "Yes, I have a sister. Would you like to meet her?"

He raised his eyebrows and shrugged.

"Her name's Diane." His long-lashed, blue eyes held mine. "She's almost four years old," I said, grinning.

Lenny chortled. "Oh, perfect."

When my parents arrived to visit, Jo introduced her son. During the lively conversation, another couple entered.

"Get out of that bed," a dark-haired man said to Jo.

"Well, hi," Jo said, holding the word like a note.

The man's arresting blue eyes twinkled merrily. "Get up and make me a sandwich."

A well-groomed lady who had accompanied the man punched him on the arm. "Jerry!"

The man jumped back. "Okay." He stepped up to Kenny, shook his hand, and then quickly gave Jo a kiss. "Hi, Mom."

"It's good to see both of you," Jo said.

"Hel-lo," the lady warbled.

After introducing her middle son, Jerry, and his wife, Carol, the noise level rose considerably as everyone in the room became acquainted.

Unexpectedly a nurse appeared in the doorway, hands on hips, and scanned the crowd. "All right, who's having a party and didn't invite me?"

Immediately Jo spoke up. "I'm sorry if we disturbed anyone. We'll try to keep the noise down."

The nurse frowned, then softened her expression. "Well, since it's Sunday, we tend to be more tolerant. I'll ignore the number of visitors." She held a finger to her lips and hurried on her way.

The two brothers leaned against the wall and poked each other, snickering like school boys caught whispering in class. Jerry's hair was longer and darker than his younger brother's, but I could see the resemblance in the eyes, the lips, and the gap between their front teeth. Jerry's upturned nose matched his mother's while Lenny's nose tended to slope downward. Each had slender fingers on their delicate hands. Although Lenny stood a couple inches taller than his brother, Jerry outweighed him by fifty pounds. Both brothers wore pressed, short-sleeve dress shirts, crisp twill slacks, and polished loafers. I could see why Jo was proud of her boys.

The afternoon sped by faster than a great movie. The two brothers bantered back and forth, even drawing smiles and chuckles from my usually reserved Dad. By dinnertime, the visitors began to take their leave, back to lives that didn't involve operations or pain. I wanted to run after them. My parents said their farewells with less fanfare than Jo's visitors, promising to return the next day.

Jo clung to her husband, then her sons. "I gotta get going," Lenny said. "I have to pick up Rosemary. I love you, and I'll see you tomorrow." He tugged on Kenny's arm, finally pulling him from the room.

In the resulting silence, Jo sighed. "That was so nice."

"You have a wonderful family," I said.

"I'm very blessed."

I absently rubbed my leg. I had hardly given it a second thought all afternoon. Lenny's jocularity had distracted me from the nagging discomfort. Just thinking about his wisecracks ignited a smile. He was not only funny but also nice-looking, especially those gorgeous eyes. Still, I thought his humor a bit sarcastic, and he clearly wasn't interested in me because he asked if I had a sister. I wondered who Rosemary was. Probably his girlfriend. Well, I was in no condition to attract his attention. I pushed aside my wayward musings with a heavy sigh just as the nurse delivered my dinner tray.

Monday started off with the usual hospital routine—doctor visit, breakfast, bed bath, wheelchair, and physical therapy. My strength and endurance increased the more I practiced with the crutches, yet my coordination faltered like a newborn colt. I couldn't be discharged until I could master steps and doors.

That afternoon Lenny paid his mom another visit. She told him the doctor planned to send her home the next day. At once I felt saddened, and I didn't know why. Was it because I wasn't going home? Or was it because I would miss Jo? Or her son? Pushing my thoughts aside, I savored the afternoon. Lenny shared stories of his military training; I shared the fact that I missed my guitar. Sometime later Lenny left the room and returned with a gift for me—a plastic toy banjo. I laughed as I tried to produce some recognizable sound from the toy, convinced Lenny thought I was totally inept.

"Did you know I'm getting a new car?" Lenny asked. "A '48 Chevy."

"Oh, that's nice," I said. "My last boyfriend also had a '48 Chevy, hand-painted grass green including brush strokes. It only had one functioning door, and the upholstery looked as if it were chewed on by rats."

Caught off-guard, Lenny smiled and shook his head. "No, I'm just kidding. I'm really getting a brand new '68 Chevelle. Maybe I'll take you for a ride sometime."

"I'd like that," I said, sounding much too eager.

"Hopefully the car will be delivered before I report back for duty."

Lenny's leave had already been extended and would end soon. He expected to be shipped back to Vietnam. Suddenly my problems seemed inconsequential.

Mom and Dad paid me a visit, and later Gina stopped by. Looking healthy and fetching in her summer short outfit, Gina batted her blue-green eyes at Lenny and giggled at all his remarks. Like Cinderella in rags, I watched the interplay that scoured my heart. When visiting hours drew to a close, Lenny said his good-byes. I didn't know if I'd ever see him again.

Gina bid me a hasty farewell. "Wait, Lenny. I'll walk out with you." She snatched up her purse and trotted after him.

*    *    *

# CHAPTER NINETEEN—MIXED EMOTIONS AND SOCKS

My roommate, Jo, stuffed the last of her things in her bag just as her husband arrived to take her home. "You be sure to call me the moment you get home. I told your mom I wanted you to visit me." Jo shuffled over and gave me a hug, then took a seat in the wheelchair the nurse held for her. "You get that crutch-walking down." She waved a good-bye and grasped Kenny's hand as the nurse wheeled her from the room.

Unbidden tears moistened my eyes. I clamped down my emotions, telling myself everything was fine.

A few minutes later a nurse rushed in the room. "Sorry, but we're going to move you to another room." She began to gather my belongings.

"Another room? Why can't I stay here?"

"We need to put men in this room," she said as she heaped my things around me in the bed.

Two nurses rolled my bed into a new room at the far end of the corridor. As I entered, I glimpsed a rooftop through the window just before they parked me in the spot closest to the door. Without a word, my new roommate closed the privacy curtain between the beds, obscuring even the poor view from the window. Again tears formed and threatened to spill over.

*I just have to get out of here.*

I telephoned Mom to tell her I'd been transferred. I wanted to cry and have her soothe my hurt, but I didn't know why I felt so sad. My secluded roommate cleared her throat and sighed loudly, so I quickly ended my call. I stuck out my tongue at the curtained wall, which somehow made me feel better.

During therapy, I worked hard learning to go up and down stairs and how to manage doors. After two lengthy sessions, I mulled over how I could persuade the doctor to discharge me in the morning. My hair hadn't been washed in a week, and I couldn't wait to scrub away the stale hospital smell. I dreamed of shaving my legs and soaking in a hot bath, yet I knew I'd have to wait until the stitches came out. I was sick of the food, sick of the routine, and sick of being sick. When Mom paid her visit, I told her I wasn't staying another day. Somehow I was going home.

After Mom left, I grudgingly kept quiet so as not to further disturb the hermit in the bed next to me. Bored, I leafed through a magazine. Unexpectedly, Lenny strolled through the doorway. I thought I had imagined him.

He wore a smile. "There you are. Trying to confuse me by changing rooms?"

I slammed the magazine shut and pushed myself upright, smoothing my covers. "What are you doing here?"

His eyes sparkled. "Thought you might miss me."

I tried to still my rapid pulse. "I sure can use the company." I nodded my head toward the closed curtain and whispered, "Not too friendly in this neck of the woods."

Lenny raised one eyebrow and quietly said, "Not very sociable, I see."

I nodded. "So, how's your mom doing at home?"

He sat in the chair near my bed. "Great. She feels pretty good. How're you doing?"

I related the highlights of my day, and we talked as easily as if we had known each other for years. Getting to know Lenny was like a ride through the fun house. I didn't know when the next quip would zing my way and tickle me. Too soon, the ride ended. I thanked Lenny for coming and told him I planned on going home tomorrow. "Tell your mom I'll call her."

"Sure." He stood to leave and glanced at the floor, then looked at me, a slight smile on his lips. "So . . . I guess I'll see you later."

The click of his loafers on the tile floor faded. I couldn't stop grinning as though I had just won a prize. For what I wasn't exactly sure. It couldn't be for beauty, style, or grace. Why had Lenny come? What about Rosemary? Was she his girlfriend? What about Gina? She chased him like a bitch in heat. Still, he did come to see me. But it didn't mean anything. He was just being nice, maybe even doing it for his mom. Besides, he had a real life with responsibilities while I was just a high school girl—with dirty hair, a red arm, and a pair of crutches.

I yanked the light cord and plunged my cubicle into darkness, hiding from myself. I flipped my pillow to the cool side and pressed my feverish cheek against it. My mind replayed Lenny's visit, and sleep eluded me for a long time.

The next morning I got my crutch-walking papers from the doctor. I couldn't wait to escape. The nurse provided me with home instructions, prescriptions, and an appointment reminder.

At last, Mom arrived with a pair of culottes and a top for me to wear home. I wrestled into my clothes, feeling one step closer to normal. An entourage of personnel accompanied me to the car, bearing bags of my belongings and pots of wilting flowers. After helping me into the passenger seat, the nurses stashed my crutches in the back and waved goodbye.

I inhaled a deep breath of hot, stuffy car air, thinking it the most pleasant smell, and exhaled with a moan of satisfaction. Mom handed me my sunglasses and then drove away from the curb as if she were transporting Waterford crystal. The warm June day resuscitated me. Flowers bloomed and lush lawns gleamed like emeralds. My head bobbed from side to side like one of those springy dogs that folks placed in their rear car windows. Things looked the same yet different. Was it just a little over a week I had been gone?

Finally, Mom eased the car in the driveway. "I think I'll park here rather than in the garage so you can get out more easily. Do you think you can manage the sidewalk?"

"I think so."

Mom helped me slide out and handed me the crutches. I took a glimpse at the house and limped off down the sidewalk. Several minutes later I hopped up the single porch step. Before Mom could open the door, it flew open, and Grandma, Grandpa, Roger, and Diane shouted greetings. Smiling, I hobbled into the living room where I collapsed on the sofa.

Sniffing back tears, I set my crutches aside and hugged everyone. "I made it."

"So you did," Grandma said. "Do you want something to eat?"

"Not right now. Thanks."

Grandpa lit his pipe and took a few puffs, coughed, and then wheezed out a laugh. "Are you gettin' around with those sticks?"

"I'm trying." I saw little Diane's eyes dart from my leg to the crutches. "Come here." She drew closer, and I wrapped my arms around her in a tight embrace. "You look like you've grown an inch. Did you miss me?" She nodded. "Well, I missed you, too."

Grandpa rose from his chair. "Come on, Luetta, let's get going."

"Oh, George," Grandma scolded.

He shuffled across the room. "Let the girl rest. She don't need your hoverin'."

Grandma grabbed her purse. "We'll see you later." She turned back to me. "You be careful not to overdo."

"I will. Thanks, Grandma."

After they left, Roger pointed toward the family room. "Do you want to watch TV?"

"No, I think I'll just sit here for a bit. It's just nice to be home. You go ahead. I'll be in later."

While Mom got busy unpacking my things, Diane brought me her dolls. I was more than happy to retreat into her make-believe world.

Mom returned to the living room with a handful of socks. "These don't look like your socks. Are these your socks?"

I shook my head.

"I bet they're Jo's. Well, I better give her a call." She left the room, but I heard her on the kitchen phone, explaining the sock mix-up to Jo. A few minutes later she announced that Jo sends her best, and tomorrow we were going to her house to return the socks.

I kept my happiness to myself, but I wanted to yell, "Way to go, Mom!" I might have another chance to see Lenny.

That afternoon Mom washed my hair. I took a thorough sponge bath, shaved my legs as best I could, and brushed my hair until it dried. When Dad came home after work, I looked more like myself. I had just enough energy to join the family at the table for dinner. Mom's cooking had never tasted so good. While she tidied the kitchen, I relaxed in the family room, but exhaustion soon sent me hobbling toward my bed.

Mom tucked me into bed as if I were Diane's age. "Now, if you want my help to get up during the night, just yell."

"I'll be fine. Thanks for everything, Mom. It's really good to be home." I kissed her. "I love you," I added as she turned off the light.

"I love you too, sweetheart." She padded off.

The scent of fabric softener wafted around me, and I snuggled deeper into my cozy bed. Sleep claimed me before I had a chance to consider what I would wear to Jo's.

Dad's noisy bathroom routine woke me early the next morning. I couldn't believe I'd slept undisturbed all night. I sat up and reached for my crutches just as Dad poked his head into my room. "Good morning, Glory."

Smiling at his familiar greeting, I replied, "Great morning."

"How'd you sleep?"

"Like a baby."

"Hungry?"

"Starving."

"Well, get a move on." He disappeared.

I launched myself off the bed and followed the smell of bacon. In her robe, Mom stood at the stove, breaking eggs into a skillet. "Good morning, sweetheart."

I slid into a chair. "Morning, Mom. That smells great."

"Have some juice. This will be ready soon. Did you sleep okay?"

"Wonderfully. No more hospital beds for me."

Dad clomped into the kitchen, dressed in his boots and work clothes, and switched on the radio before he took his seat at the table. "So, what's on the a-genda today?" he asked, emphasizing the "a."

Mom popped two slices of bread into the toaster. "We're going to Jo's to return her socks that got mixed in with Debbie's."

Dad grinned and shook his head. "Already going gallivanting around town."

I fiddled with my napkin. "Just to Jo's. It's a little hard to gallivant on crutches."

Mom handed us plates of food. "Don't worry, Don. We won't be staying out long."

Dad meticulously cut his bacon and eggs. "I know how you women can get to talking."

Mom frowned and shook her head. "I was thinking Debbie might enjoy a brief outing, and this afternoon she might want to sit out by the pool and enjoy the sunshine."

I buttered my toast. "That sounds good. My suntan has already faded."

"What about Roger and Diane?" Dad asked between mouthfuls.

Mom sat down. "I promised them they could swim this afternoon."

Dad chuckled, and I knew he was thinking that Diane wouldn't go in the pool. But she braved the inflatable wading pool that sat on the deck.

Dad scraped up the last of his food. "Well, you girls have a nice visit." He took his empty plate to the sink and then stomped back to the bathroom.

After Dad left for work, Roger and Diane finally awoke and ate breakfast. I freshened up and got dressed. My stomach felt a little queasy, either from the eggs or from the hope that Lenny would be home when I visited his mom.

*    *    *

# CHAPTER TWENTY—FIVE DAYS

Mom steered the car into a guest parking space alongside a small apartment complex in the west end of town. My nerves strained with anticipation. I squeezed the hand grips of my crutches and negotiated the three steps leading up to the walkway. Mom rang the bell, and Lenny greeted us with a big smile. "Hi, come on in."

"Good morning," Jo called from her chair in the living room. "Have a seat." She watched me poke my way toward the sofa. "You're doing pretty good there."

With a sigh, I sat down. "I'm learning." I searched for a spot to stow my crutches.

Lenny stepped forward. "Let me get those out of your way."

I looked into his bewitching eyes and tried not to stammer. "Thank you."

He stashed the crutches in the corner. "Can I get you ladies something to drink?"

"Water will be fine," I said.

"Same for me." Mom returned Jo's socks and took a seat at the opposite end of the sofa.

Lenny excused himself to the kitchen, and the two mothers began to chatter as if they hadn't seen each other in years. I glanced around the tidy apartment, tastefully decorated in earth tones. Decorative orange accent bowls and vases gleamed on polished wooden tables, and slender lamps cast soft, inviting glows. Tall brass candlesticks stood on either side of a console television which was adorned with studio portraits of Jo's sons. Jo occupied one of two occasional chairs, and I suspected the recliner was Kenny's domain. A painting of a Spanish senorita graced one wall. To my right, I could see the edge of the dining room that led, I presumed, to the kitchen. On my left, a hallway trailed toward the bedrooms.

Lenny returned and handed Mom and me our drinks. "Here you go."

He sat on the edge of the recliner and looked at me. "So, what's it like to be home?"

My mouth dry, I took a sip and placed my glass in a crystal coaster on the table. "It's wonderful." I babbled about my tiny milestones, yet Lenny didn't seem to mind the topic. An affable host, he listened and smiled and made me feel right at home.

All too soon Mom brought the visit to a close. Lenny fetched my crutches. As I stood up and tried to cram them under my arms, dizziness overtook me. I swayed to my right.

Before I could crash to the floor, Lenny shot out a hand and grabbed my arm to steady me.

I chuckled, certain my cheeks were flushed from embarrassment. "I guess I'm not as good with these as I thought."

When I had regained my balance, Lenny released his hold on my arm. "Just takes a little practice." He hovered near me while I made my way to the door and said good-bye.

On the way home, I cringed, remembering how I had swooned like a southern belle with an attack of the vapors. I had wanted to impress Lenny, but I probably scared him off. I doubted he had time to waste on a lame school girl. He had told me he was leaving Tuesday for California to await his orders back to Vietnam. I was sure he had better things to do with his last five days of liberty than babysit me.

The next morning, however, Lenny surprised me with a phone call. "What can you do?"

Did he mean what my parents allowed me to do? Or was he asking if I could do more tricks like falling over on my crutches. "What do you mean, 'What can I do?'"

"Like . . . go somewhere or something?"

"Well, I'm still not too great with these crutches." I hoped I hadn't discouraged him.

"How about taking a drive?"

"Great. I can do that."

My parents agreed to the "date." For the rest of the day, I hummed while I primped. To add interest to my bland crutches, I wound yards of orange and pink ribbon around them to match the outfit I chose—orange culottes and a pink, white, and orange-striped shirt. I don't know what I was thinking, wearing orange when the color so obviously clashed with my red arm.

Right on time, Lenny rang the doorbell. After a quick hello to my folks, he walked me to the car with his hand near my elbow, perhaps anticipating another near tumble. "Sorry for the wheels," he said. "My new car should arrive tomorrow. This is my parents' car."

I eased inside the roomy Chevy sedan. "Nothing wrong with this."

Lenny steered the car north out of the city. "I thought I'd show you where I grew up."

We entered Collinsville, a small city north of Belleville. Like a tour guide, Lenny showed me where his brother and sister-in-law now resided and where he and his brothers had lived when they were young. He entertained me with stories of his old friends and neighbors. When he turned the car into a park off Main Street, he directed my attention to a lake nestled at the bottom of a hill. "There's where I learned to swim."

"Really? In a lake?"

He laughed. "Yes. It was the sink or swim approach. My buddies dragged me out to the middle, and I had to get back on my own. I kind of dog-paddled and swallowed a lot of water, but I made it to the bank."

"I never tried that method with the kids I taught, but it's tempting."

"Eventually, I did learn some strokes."

Lenny guided the car out of the shady park, back to the highway, and headed north again. Leaving Collinsville behind, we talked while he drove past acres of farmland that were dotted with stands of trees clustered around weathered houses. I studied his profile and watched him drive. His slender fingers caressed the wheel with a familiarity I found reassuring. I happened to notice a brown birthmark on the back of his right wrist. He hadn't mentioned my birthmark. Wearing a sleeveless top, I hadn't bothered to hide mine.

We entered the town of Edwardsville. "This is where we lived when I was born. I was pretty young, but I think I can find the house where we lived." He cruised up and down side streets, scanning the names. "There it is." He pulled the car to the curb in front of a shotgun house. "It sure hasn't changed much."

"What a peaceful neighborhood. Do you remember much?"

"Walking to school. Hanging out with my friends." He stared at the house. "I lived here with my grandma, aunt, and brothers, and we didn't have air conditioning." He swiped his brow.

"We didn't have air conditioning, either. I hated having the windows open because I was afraid someone would slit the screen and get me."

"Funny you should say that. I remember my brothers and I had accidentally sent a softball through that front window, and it left a big hole in the glass. The bed Jerry and I shared was right under the broken window. One night, before we had gotten the window repaired, we were sleeping, and an arm came through the hole and poked Jerry. He woke up screaming. That woke me and I screamed."

"Oh, my goodness. What did you do?"

He snickered. "Nothing. We realized it was Mom. She had forgotten her key and was trying to wake us up to open the door."

Lenny shook his head, and we laughed. He put the car in gear. As night overtook dusk, he started south toward home.

I was sorry when he pulled the car into my driveway.

"Here you are, safe and sound."

"Thanks for the drive. It was just what the doctor ordered." I waited while he came around the car to open my door.

Before Lenny and I reached the porch, Mom dashed out of the house with her camera in hand. "I just want to get a picture, real quick."

I looked at Lenny. Amusement brightened his eyes, and I scowled at my mother. "Oh, Mom."

She raised the camera. "Come on. It will only take a second."

Against the black background of night, I hunched over my crutches and placed one arm loosely around Lenny's narrow waist. He gently laid his hand on my back, and we both grinned.

"Say 'Cheese.'" Mom snapped the picture and ducked back inside.

Blinded by the flash, I finished my trek to the door, toward that awkward moment. "Well, I had a lovely time."

"Me, too." Lenny opened the front door for me and made sure I hopped safely into the house. When I pivoted to say good-bye, Lenny thrust out his hand. "Well, good night then."

I extended my hand, and he grasped it, but instead of shaking it, he bent over it and kissed it like a prince bidding his lady good night. Without a word, he disappeared into the dark.

I closed the door. That certainly was different. Nevertheless, I floated to bed between my crutches. I felt warm inside as if I had just enjoyed a cup of cocoa and a cookie. Could Lenny be interested in me? I wanted to believe he was, but I didn't want to get my hopes up.

The next day I spoke with my friends and caught up on the latest teen happenings. Naturally, I talked to Bobby, who couldn't wait to intrude on my recovery. I chatted with Gina and mentioned that Lenny and I had seen each other a couple times. She was unusually silent about the news, but I attributed her mood to another disagreement with Mark.

That afternoon Lenny dropped by, arriving in his brand new car. "I thought maybe you'd like to go for a spin."

"You bet." I hobbled outside to find a 1968, ash-gold Chevelle shining like new money. "Wow, that's a beautiful car."

With a wide smile, Lenny opened the long passenger door, and I slipped into the bucket seat. He put my crutches in the back, then jumped in and cranked the engine. The dual mufflers rumbled like a jet before takeoff, but Lenny teased the car out of the drive and up the road.

I inhaled the new car scent and watched Lenny fiddle with the controls like a pilot. He jabbed an eight-track tape in the stereo, and Junior Walker's voice singing "Shotgun" surrounded me. "Cool. This is really nice. When did you get the car?"

"Just picked it up. Look, it only has three miles on it." He pointed to a gauge.

I leaned over the center console to peek at the odometer. "Three miles." *He must have come right over from the dealer's.* I smiled. *He gave me the first ride.* My hopes soared. "Very new."

"Yes. I'm still figuring out the controls."

We cruised Main Street almost to his house, then turned around to head back. Although the ride was brief, I bubbled with happiness.

Lenny laughed as he helped me from the sporty car. "Not quite a '48 Chevy."

"Not at all. You have fine taste in cars."

He stepped closer to me. "Would you like to go out tomorrow night? See how she runs?"

"I'd love to . . . as long as it doesn't involve walking."

"Okay. How about dinner and a movie?"

"Sounds wonderful."

He escorted me to the door and said good-bye. He practically skipped back to his car like a kid who couldn't wait to ride his new bike. Gliding into the kitchen, I told Mom that Lenny had asked me to dinner and a movie.

"Isn't that sweet?" She turned back to her dishes.

I thought Saturday night would never arrive. Lenny drove us to the Fox Theater in St. Louis where we saw *The Green Berets*, a John Wayne film about the war in Vietnam. I liked the movie, but it also frightened me, knowing that Lenny had to return to the war. I looked at him differently, visualizing the soldier.

After the movie, we shared a pizza at a fancy Italian restaurant. In the car, before leaving for home, Lenny turned toward me and gave me a tender kiss. He grinned and licked his lips. "Mmm, pizza breath."

I laughed, but I wanted to sing. When he walked me to my door, he kissed me again. "Would you like to come over tomorrow? You could swim if you like."

He glanced at my leg. "What about you?"

"I can't swim, but I can sit by the pool."

"Okay, it's a date."

Lenny didn't swim the next day, but we sat by the pool and talked and talked. Later, Mom invited him to stay for dinner. He joked with my brother and sister, behaved politely toward my parents, and demonstrated proper table manners.

Monday, Lenny and I took in a drive-in movie.

On Tuesday morning, Lenny showed up at the house with a gift for me. I tore off the wrapping paper to find a slim black box. Inside was a key ring with two keys. "To my car," he said when I frowned at him. "While I'm gone, drive the car anytime you want."

I felt tears welling in my eyes, but I sniffed them back. "That's so nice of you, but I doubt I'll be doing much driving, at least for a little while." I gave him a half smile.

"Well, I guess I'll get going. My flight leaves in a few hours."

"You take care. Write when you can."

"I will." He hugged and kissed me one last time.

As fast as he came into my life, he was gone. He trusted me enough with the keys to his new car, but that didn't imply a relationship. He had four months of military service left to complete, and a lot could happen, a lot of scary things.

*     *     *

# CHAPTER TWENTY-ONE—LOVE LETTERS

"Debbie, phone for you," Mom shouted from the kitchen.

I hobbled from my room and grabbed the hall extension. "Hello."

"Hi there."

Hearing the familiar voice, my heart stuttered, and my spirits rose like helium balloons. "Lenny! Where are you?"

"In California, a base in Oakland. Say, did you borrow my car?"

"No."

"Well, I didn't think so, but I thought I'd check. Mom told me she had to report my car stolen."

"Stolen! Your new car? How awful."

Lenny sighed. "Yeah, I can't believe it. Only a week old. But at least it was insured. The police told Mom that if they find it, it'll most likely have been stripped for parts."

The phone cord uncoiled as I limped into my room and sat on my bed. "What are you going to do?"

"Order another car." He chuckled.

"Great idea."

"Do you miss me?" he asked in a softer voice.

My eyes flitted to my vanity where the snapshot Mom took of Lenny and me stood propped against the mirror. "Yes, I haven't been anywhere since you left, except to the doctor. I had my stitches removed."

"That's good. Now you can swim, right?"

"Yes, sort of. Floating around in an inner tube isn't my idea of swimming."

"Beats typing."

"Typing?"

"That's what they have me doing right now. I met a sergeant who was born and raised in Belleville. Can you believe that? When I told him I was headed back to 'Nam, he suggested I request stateside duty. He said the request would be denied, but by the time it was processed, I would be short."

"What does that mean?"

"Having less than sixty days to serve. The army can't send short-timers overseas."

"Wow! That'd be great."

"He's a good guy. I'm doing the typing for him."

I fiddled with the phone cord. "Can I write to you?"

"I don't have an address, yet. As soon as I do, I'll let you know." He was silent for a moment. "Well, I better get going . . ."

"I'm glad you called, but I'm so sorry your car was stolen."

"Yeah, thanks. You take care. I'll talk to you later."

"You be careful, too. Bye." I hugged the receiver as if I could hold onto him a little longer. My face hurt from smiling, and I would have skipped if I wasn't on crutches.

Mom came around the corner after I had replaced the receiver. "Lenny?"

"Yes." I stopped smiling. "His new car was stolen. He was making sure I hadn't borrowed it."

"Did they find it?"

"Not yet."

She shook her head and marched off, keeping to her household schedule.

A couple days later I got a letter from Lenny. The red and blue-edged airmail envelope, dated July 18, bore no return address, but it was postmarked from Oakland, California. I opened the envelope as if it were a birthday present. Lenny's handwriting, scrawled on two pages, tickled me as I read. He signed "Love Lenny" and added two postscripts. In the first, he offered to take me out twice a day, and in the second he asked, "Don't I write stupid letters?" No, I thought, he wrote to me, despite my red skin and hobbling gait. He signed it "Love." Did he really feel affection for me? I was afraid to hope.

The next day, I got another envelope from Lenny, a brief note also signed, "Love." He'd written a poem on the back of the paper. When I finished reading the poem, tears moistened my eyes. I never knew he could be so sensitive. There was a lot I didn't know about him, and I couldn't wait to learn more.

The letters kept arriving, sometimes two at a time. I felt terrible I couldn't write back. Lenny managed to make me smile, yet I knew he was worried about going back to Vietnam. I couldn't ease his loneliness or fears until he gave me his address. Finally, on July 25, Jo called with the information. I couldn't wait for her to hang up so I could send Lenny one of the letters I had ready to mail.

Lenny and I began a proper correspondence. I told him I'd given Gina his address because I knew she would ask Jo for it if I didn't tell her. She said she wanted to write to someone, but I suspected something was up. At the end of July, Lenny confirmed my suspicions. He admitted he had taken Gina out the night he got his new car, but he assured me he wasn't interested in her. He wrote that he cared only for me.

I knew it! That Gina! In her "off again" mode with Mark, she had targeted Lenny, launched her ammunition, and cared not if her spray of bullets wounded a bystander. During her break with Mark last spring, I had gone with Mark and two couples to a baseball game. Although Gina knew about it and knew it was totally innocent, she must have felt I betrayed her, so she had evened the score.

I couldn't blame Lenny for asking her out. She was petite, cute, and bubbly. I reread the letter. Lenny claimed he was interested in me, that he cared, and he had signed it "Love," again. He asked me not to say anything to Gina, so I kept my mouth shut about their date. However, in the back of my mind, I wondered if Lenny simply couldn't decide which one of us he wanted.

While I pined for Lenny and pretended all was fine, the girls—Nell, her friend Helen, and, of course, Gina—joined me afternoons at the pool, sometimes bringing Bobby with them. They swam while I bobbed in the inner tube. Nell and Helen wanted to hear all about Lenny. The more I talked about him, the quieter Gina became and the more antagonistic Bobby got.

"Lenny, Lenny, Lenny. That's all I hear. Big time soldier," Bobby grumbled.

I splashed water on his red head. "Oh, knock it off."

Bobby swiped water from his face and moved to the side of the pool. "Bet he has a cool car, too."

"He did. It was just stolen, but I think he's going to order another one."

Bobby leaned back against the wall and rested his elbows on the coping and muttered, "Figures."

As the days crawled by, Lenny and I counted down the days he had left in the army, and by the middle of August, he wrote he was under sixty days.

He wasn't going to Vietnam!

He was reassigned to Fort Sheridan in Chicago. Although closer to me, his duty assignment prevented him from traveling down state to see me. But his letters promised he would try to get away soon to visit me.

I started my senior year on crutches. My friends helped carry my books and guard me while I hopped up and down flights of stairs. Naturally, Bobby got involved, probably just to pester me since he couldn't annoy me in band. I missed being in the marching band, but I had the good fortune of joining the yearbook staff. Gina, also on the staff, had recently rekindled her relationship with Mark, and I rejoiced.

Throughout September, Lenny's letters continued with regularity. He wrote that he planned to get a job and go to college after his discharge. He was concerned about our four-year age difference. He had just turned twenty-one and I seventeen. For me, it wasn't a problem. Lenny didn't act any older than me, yet the four-year difference polished him so he sparkled brighter than boys my age. His compliments made me feel like Cinderella at the ball. When he professed his love, I reciprocated. I couldn't think of anyone except him.

Finally, one October day, Lenny came to my door, a civilian again after two years in the Army. "I can't believe you're here." I threw my arms around his neck and never wanted to let go.

Lenny pulled far enough away to look at me. "Only one crutch?"

"Yes, I can almost walk without it. Won't be long, I'll be dancing."

Lenny began his job search and waited for his new car to arrive while I concentrated on school work and ridding myself of the last crutch. At the end of the month, I cast it aside. No longer bogged down by walking problems, I enjoyed every spare minute with Lenny. I wasn't too sure my parents approved of our dating, but they didn't forbid me to see him. They couldn't complain about my attitude because a smile lit my face every day.

By Christmas, Lenny had his new 1969 Chevelle, nearly identical to the previous model. He had accepted a position in customer service at the Westinghouse Corporation in St. Louis. When I saw him in his three-piece suit and tie, he looked so dashing, I wanted to show him off to the world, proclaim him as my boyfriend. I remembered Jane's prophecy from my yearbook, "Maybe some great changes will come this summer." She was so right.

With Lenny commuting to St. Louis for his job, I wasn't able to see him as often as I liked, but we made the most of the weekends. I dragged him to school basketball games; he took me to dinners and movies. When the winter formal dance at school drew near, Lenny happily agreed to go with me.

"You look beautiful," Lenny whispered as we posed for Mom's pictures, dressed in our formal attire.

"Thank you. You're very fetching yourself." I drank in his handsome figure. His short, military haircut had grown into a longer style, and a few extra pounds banished the gaunt jungle-look he had when we met.

Mom pinned the black orchid Lenny had chosen on the cut-velvet gown she had sewed for me. She stepped back to admire me. "Perfect."

The white, empire waist dress, accented with a black velvet ribbon at the bodice and white ostrich feathers at the neck, made me look like a snowflake. I wagged my banana-curled head and then twirled in a circle, careful not to fall or step on my hem. "So, how do I look?"

"Beautiful," Mom said.

Lenny smiled, his blue eyes the only hint of color highlighting his tall, dark, and handsome appearance. "I agree. You're perfect. Well, shall we get going?"

Perfect? No one had ever referred to me as perfect. For once, I felt normal. My red and purple skin was forgotten.

Dad offered a small smile as Lenny and I left. "Be careful."

The dance, my first formal affair since the sorority event, was as wonderful as I had imagined. I discovered Lenny was a good dancer. Secure in his arms, his delicate fingers laced in mine, I floated across the floor and gazed up at him. Although I wore one-inch heels, he towered head and shoulders above me. He bent low and murmured endearments as we rocked to "Hey Jude," which we laughingly deemed "our song." At the end of the evening, I knew for certain he was my prince.

\*      \*      \*

# CHAPTER TWENTY-TWO—LIFE DECISIONS

I brooded in my room one winter day. What was I going to do with my life? I wanted to marry Lenny after graduating from high school, but I knew my parents wouldn't agree to that. Spending four years in college seemed pointless without any notion of what I would do with that education. I didn't aspire to be a teacher like my friends, but I supposed I should have some sort of job. Mom encouraged me to become a dental assistant, yet the thought of people drooling and spitting disgusted me. Dad voted for college.

I flirted with the idea of becoming a nurse. Two of my aunts were nurses. Both still worked but had taken breaks to have children. That might be nice because I hoped to have kids one day. Nurses were in demand and had a lot of employment choices—hospitals, medical offices, schools, nursing homes, state agencies, even the military—and numerous options within each choice. St. Louis had a half dozen nursing schools with two and three year programs that cost a fraction of college tuition. That should make my parents happy. Attending school in St. Louis would keep me close to home and close to Lenny. Nursing sounded better and better to me. Besides, I'd look great in a cute white uniform and starched cap.

After thoroughly researching the various schools, I decided that Jewish Hospital School of Nursing best suited me. I informed my parents of my decision. Although they didn't veto nursing school, each argued their choice. I promised to think about their suggestions.

Days later, Mom brought up the subject again, suddenly siding with Dad. "You *can* go to college to study nursing . . . at Southern Illinois University, Edwardsville."

I looked up from my homework spread across the kitchen table. "And train at St. Mary's in East St. Louis? It's not even safe to drive through that city. You know, a nurse doesn't need a college degree to get a job. I don't want to spend four years in college."

Mom rattled a skillet out of the cupboard. "You just want to be near Lenny."

"I want to be a nurse. What does that have to do with Lenny? And what's so wrong with him?"

She banged down the skillet on the stove. "You would meet lots of boys in college."

"I met lots of boys in high school, but they never called me. Lenny loves me. Maybe I should marry him and forget school." With a flick of my head, I whipped my long hair behind my ears and glared in her direction.

Mom wheeled toward me, the spoon in her hand beating the air. "Now don't get smart with me, young lady. Your father and I just want the best for you." She checked the waving spoon. "And we think you're too young to be tied down with one boy . . . man."

"I'm going to apply to Jewish." I snatched up my books and stomped off to my room, slamming the door with my backside.

I tossed my books onto the bed and paced the room. Other boys! Boys used to tease me because of my birthmark. Later, they ignored me or simply tolerated me. Then I met Lenny, and he didn't care that I was different. What was wrong with Mom? Didn't she see I wasn't like other girls? I was lucky to have a boyfriend. And now she wanted to keep us apart. Any mother would be happy her daughter had such a kind, respectful, responsible boyfriend. Any mother would be proud her daughter wanted to be a nurse. I flipped on the radio and plopped down on the bed, letting the music cut off my spiraling thoughts.

*     *     *

"I got accepted to Jewish!" I squealed on the phone to Lenny some months later.

"Way to go. I knew you would."

His support touched me. "I can't believe I start in September."

"My little nurse," he teased.

"I hope I can walk okay by then. You know I'm having the rod removed from my leg before school starts. Dr.

Haydon said it was a simple surgery, so I should be up and around by the next day."

"Do you want me to come visit you again?"

"You bet. It'll be like old times."

The remainder of my senior year dwindled to an end. Soon after I played "Go Where You Want to Go" on my guitar at the Senior Hootenanny, I attended my first prom. Lenny and I double dated with Mark and Gina, indiscretions of the past all forgotten. The yearbook was finished, and I was proud to have participated in its evolution. Finally, graduation. No longer facing an uncertain future, I embraced my life plan, eager for the next phase. My parents also seemed happy with my decision to go to nursing school, relieved I wasn't eloping with Lenny.

Late August of 1969 was a season of new beginnings. Not only was I starting nursing school, but my brother was beginning high school and my sister entering kindergarten. Mom was going crazy attending to all the details, not to mention taking time out when I had my surgery. Then, with tears in her eyes, she helped me gather the things I would take with me to school.

Approximately ten miles west of Lenny's office in downtown St. Louis, Jewish Hospital School of Nursing was tucked between Jewish Hospital and Children's Hospital, bordered by Washington University, Barnes Hospital, and the St. Louis College of Pharmacy. The school faced the eastern edge of Forest Park, site of the 1904 World's Fair, now a handy playground for the hoard of medical personnel in the area. For two and a half years, the neighborhood was my world. Nursing opened my eyes to its world, one I found fascinating and rewarding.

During my pediatric rotation, I satisfied my own curiosity about birthmarks while researching the subject for a class assignment. Although the exact cause was unknown, I learned that vascular anomalies were divided into two main types—hemangiomas and vascular malformations. A hemangioma, a benign tumor consisting of a mass of blood vessels, usually shrinks and disappears. A vascular malformation, caused by a developmental error in the blood vessels before birth, never regresses. I concluded my birthmark was a vascular malformation because it never changed. To date, treatments were largely experimental, not that I was thinking along those lines. I had learned to live with a birthmark and accepted my difference.

One of my nursing instructors said to me, "You have a great attitude. You never seem ashamed or resentful because of your birthmark. People whose bodies have been altered because of birth defects, disease, or trauma sometimes experience low self-esteem or more severe psychological problems. You have high self-esteem and such a positive attitude. You're a real inspiration to others."

Although I had come to terms with my birthmark, Lenny had trouble dealing with the comments people made. One day, a woman approached me while Lenny and I were shopping. She grasped her chest and stared at me. "Oh, my God, what happened to you?"

For a moment, I thought I'd been injured, and then I realized she was asking about my birthmark. "Oh, this is just my birthmark."

"I thought you'd been burned," the woman said.

I had heard that before, along with, "It's so big," or "Can't you get rid of it?" People pointed to me, gasped aloud, and sometimes fled, but I just attributed their behavior to ignorance. Lenny frowned, but I smiled at the woman. "No. I was born with a birthmark." I grabbed Lenny's arm and moved us away from the woman before she, like many others, tried to show me her birthmark.

"Why didn't you tell her it was none of her business?" he asked.

"I'm used to the reactions. Maybe she'll learn something."

"She should learn to keep her mouth shut," he grumbled.

By the set of his jaw, I could tell he hurt for me. Learning how to deal with my difference was new for him, yet I had to commend his restraint. He wrapped an arm around my shoulders to shield me, not understanding that I could handle the remarks.

When I finished nursing school in January, 1972, Lenny's engagement ring sparkled on my left hand. We planned to marry in April. Bobby came by my house to offer, I thought, his congratulations. Instead, he tried to dissuade me from marrying Lenny. "Marry me," he said. "I'll give you anything you want."

I hadn't realized the depth of Bobby's affection for me. "I love Lenny. And I'm going to marry him." I saw sadness in his brown eyes. "You'll always be my friend," I reminded him.

After I passed the state boards, I proudly added "RN" behind my name. My girlfriends were still in college by the time I began my first job. Hired to work on the orthopedic unit, I started my career at the hospital where I had my leg surgery. The bow-tie-wearing Dr. Haydon still practiced.

When he saw me in my cap and white uniform, he seemed a little surprised but pleased I was walking so straight.

Lenny married me on a mild April evening. Gina, my maid of honor, and four bridesmaids, two junior bridesmaids, five groomsmen, two ring bearers, family, and more than two hundred guests witnessed our vows. The lavish reception lasted through the wee morning hours, and then Lenny and I boarded a plane—my first airplane flight. Starting with a romantic week in the Pocono Mountains of Pennsylvania, we began the "happily ever after."

*     *     *

Time sped by like a tape on fast forward. When Lenny and I weren't working, we enjoyed weekends on our boat, holidays and vacations with our families, and leisure time with friends, including Mark and Gina, who eventually married. Lenny's folks had taken jobs as portrait consultants for a company that created church pictorial directories. They had given up their apartment to travel to various churches around the country. Lenny's brother, Jerry, had joined the Secret Service shortly after Lenny and I were married, and he and his family had moved to the D.C. area.

Influenced by Jerry, Lenny had been studying law enforcement at the local college. One day, he saw a flyer announcing tryouts for a play, and he went to a casting call. He got the lead role in the comedy, "What the Butler Saw." I knew my husband was funny, but he surprised me with his acting talent. During rehearsals, Lenny became friends with Rob, a lead member of the cast. Both were the same age and Vietnam veterans, and they had the same crazy sense of humor. One play led to another, and then Lenny and Rob formed an improvisational group that performed at dinner theaters.

Lenny and I had been married almost five years, and I was thinking about starting a family. Before I could discuss my desire with Lenny, he shocked me with plans of his own.

"What would you say about moving to California?" he asked me one cold afternoon.

"California?"

"Yes. I was thinking about trying my luck in Hollywood."

"You've got to be kidding!"

"I want to be a comedian. What better place than Hollywood?"

A million excuses ripped through my mind but not one valid enough to squelch my husband's dreams. "Where did this idea come from?"

Lenny looked down. "Well, Rob's thinking of going out there."

"I knew it. What are you two dreaming up?"

He braved a look at me. "Nothing. But nothing's happening around here. Nobody gets discovered in Belleville."

"So, you think Hollywood is the next step?"

"Tinsel town, baby. 'California Dreaming.'" He danced around the living room.

I smiled and shook my head. "I can't believe this."

He collapsed on the sofa beside me and grabbed my hands. "Will you come with me?" He cocked his head and blinked rapidly, his long lashes charming me.

"I don't know what to say." Would he go without me, I wondered.

"Say, 'Yes.'" He grinned like a child.

"You want to move there?"

"Yeah, I guess so. It'll probably take time to get a gig."

I sat still, though excitement teased me toward a decision. "I'm not moving unless I can get a nursing license in California without taking those tough state boards again."

"Okay, that's fair. Check it out, and then we can decide."

"About what? You going off to Hollywood alone if I can't get reciprocity?"

He shook his head. "No, no. I don't want to go without you."

"You mean about selling the mobile home and the boat and one of the cars?"

"I guess so. Look, I've got to run, but I'll be home after class. We'll talk more." He gave me a quick kiss and barged out the door.

I groaned and picked up Bubbles, our beagle mutt, and stroked her caramel-colored coat. There went my plan to start a family. What would my parents think? *Crazy*—that's what. Still, it was an interesting idea. I wasn't fond of my present nursing position, my fourth job in five years. Not a very good record. Nine months orthopedic, two years office nursing, nine months geriatric, and for the last two years neurology/ortho at a different hospital. The money was good, but the hours were terrible. I felt restless again. Maybe California would be a good change. Scary though. I ruffled the dog's ears and set her back on the floor.

*　　*　　*

# California Dreams

## CHAPTER TWENTY-THREE—EXPECTATION

Sunbeams permeated smudged living room windows that needed a good washing before the new drapes arrived. I disregarded the pressing chore; instead, I basked in the recliner, feet elevated, and stole a moment of time. Watching dust motes swim in the light, I couldn't believe Len, as he now liked to be called, and I had been living in California for more than five years. Like a passenger on a speeding train, I had been observing the scenery whiz by, not truly appreciating its wonder. For a change, it felt good to pause as if I could slow the momentum.

My loud sigh echoed in the sparsely furnished room. When was the new sofa being delivered? I better check my personal planner. I wasn't doing a very good job living up to my reputation as an organized person. I wasn't doing much of anything, sitting in my living room in the middle of the day. Sleeping all day was my habit. Steady night shifts for the past five years had turned me into a bat. I stretched and wriggled into another position.

Although comfortable, I knew I couldn't dawdle. I had to clean the house, wash the new baby clothes, and decide on a pediatrician. Glancing at my rounded abdomen, I wondered just when the baby would be born. Not yet, I hoped. It was too soon.

Just a few more weeks. Then I'd be enjoying the newly decorated house with my baby in my arms. I shifted the recliner into a sitting position and heaved myself up. With one hand on the wall for balance, I waddled along, hoping to get something accomplished before Len came home and we had to leave for our Lamaze class.

Although I had planned to work until I went into labor, a weakness in my left leg forced me to start my maternity leave six weeks before my due date. At first, I thought the pregnancy might have been aggravating my old leg surgery, but my right leg weakened, too. Then, I felt fleeting pins and needles sensations from my waist to my toes. Walking was a struggle. I hefted my heavy feet and uncooperative legs as if I had sand-weighted shoes and bones made of rubber. Fearing I'd fall and injure the baby, I had stopped working the previous week after my hospital family threw me a baby shower. I figured I just needed a rest.

*    *    *

"Breathe," Len coached. "Good . . . now relax . . . slow your breathing."

"I sure hope I'll be this relaxed when the actual time comes," I whispered from my recumbent position. Len and I were nearing the end of our Lamaze classes, and so far, he had held up well.

"Okay, that's it for tonight," the instructor announced. "I'll see you next week, and don't forget to bring your pillows."

I held out my arms to Len. "Help me up."

"Sure, dear." He pulled me to my feet. "How come all these other women can get off the floor without help?"

"They all look younger than me. But my left leg is weaker. I mentioned it to the doctor last week, but he didn't seem too concerned. And you know how cautious he is."

Len gathered up our pillows, and we headed to the car. As we were crossing the parking lot, I suddenly stumbled forward, losing control of my feet and legs. Since I had been hanging onto Len's arm like a romantic old lady, I didn't fall face first onto the asphalt.

Len steadied me. "What the hell? You're calling the doctor, immediately. You can hardly walk!"

Maybe I had been deceiving myself, but I refused to think something was wrong. Maybe other pregnant women experienced walking difficulties. Maybe the baby was pressing on a nerve. Maybe, maybe, maybe.

The next day I voiced my concern to Dr. Alverez, my obstetrician, who immediately referred me to a neurologist. Holding Len's arm, I hobbled in for a neurological examination. I knew Dr. Ladisky from the hospital. When he entered the room and first glimpsed me on his exam table, he took a step back. From his puzzled expression, I didn't think he had treated many pregnant patients.

After obtaining my past and present medical history, Dr. Ladisky examined me. I was shocked I couldn't distinguish which of my toes he touched. He used a pin to test sensation from my feet up to my knees, thighs, and abdomen. As if he were touching me with his finger, the pin pricks felt dull on my legs but sharper near my bulging waist. The doctor also checked my balance and strength. Like a drunk, I weaved a crooked path across the room, both legs markedly weak.

Dr. Ladisky straightened his small, wire-framed glasses and frowned as he dropped his reflex hammer and pin into the pocket of his starched lab coat. "Why the hell did you wait so long to come in?"

I dragged my fingers through my short highlighted hair. "Well, I suppose I thought walking was somewhat different during pregnancy."

"Not this different." He folded his arms across his chest. "I recommend you enter the hospital immediately for further tests. Let me talk with Dr. Alverez, and I'll be right back."

I tugged on my clothes, remembering when I'd worked on the neurology unit. I knew doctors routinely favored the myelogram, an x-ray of the spinal cord and the surrounding area after an injection of a radiopaque dye, as a useful diagnostic test, and I understood the risks involved. The lumbar puncture performed to introduce the dye was uncomfortable, and the acrobatic routine during the dye injection often guaranteed a patient a headache. The procedure frightened me, and I hoped I'd never need one.

Dr. Ladisky returned with Len a few minutes later. The doctor told us he had spoken with Dr. Alverez, who agreed more diagnostic tests were needed to determine the cause of my weakness and diminished sensation.

"I want you to go directly to the hospital," Dr. Ladisky said. "I've arranged for a neurosurgeon to see you. I'll be in touch with him and catch up with you later." His tall, thin form glided out of the room.

Pulling on my professional attitude for Len's sake, I harnessed my surging panic. Len was silent as he dispatched me to the hospital faster than an express delivery letter.

Arriving at St. Joseph's, I embraced the familiar surroundings amid the uncertainty of my condition. After enduring the admitting process, I was wheeled to the fourth floor west wing, the orthopedic and neurology unit. I had barely settled in bed when an appealing young man entered the room. He introduced himself as Dr. Larkin, the neurosurgeon. His winsome smile and pleasant accent, possibly South American, soothed me, but he didn't look old enough to be a doctor.

Len retreated to the far corner of the room while I related my history and symptoms and underwent a second neurologic examination. The dark-haired doctor studied the birthmark on my arm and back as if it were under the microscope. "Have you noticed any changes in your hemangioma?"

I wanted to correct his terminology and tell him I had a vascular malformation, but I held my tongue. Instead, I pointed to my right shoulder. "I've noticed these bumps seem bigger. A plastic surgeon once told me they were little aneurysms (dilatations of the walls of blood vessels), and they might enlarge or occur more readily as I get older. When I was very young, I never had any, but I had one bump when I was a teenager. Now, I seem to sprout a couple more each year." I didn't tell him about voodoo woman's cure for the wart/bump.

The doctor tore himself away from my fascinating bump. "I understand you are a nurse here."

"Yes, I'm an administrative supervisor."

"It helps that you are a nurse, so you can understand the technical language." He jotted notes. "I want to schedule a myelogram as soon as possible to find out what's going on."

*Oh no, not the dreaded myelogram.*

"I perform the procedure in radiology." He smiled and glanced shyly at my pregnant form. "Of course, we will take precautions for the baby." He explained the procedure and risks while fear coursed through my numb body. "Do you have any questions?"

"What about a CAT scan instead?"

"We might need to do that, too. But first the myelogram. It's more definitive. You have something compressing your spinal cord. Before you do further damage to the cord, we need to determine exactly where the problem is in order to begin treatment."

While Dr. Larkin droned on about nerve roots and intervertebral disc spaces, I tried to dredge up entombed knowledge from a decade-old anatomy class. Ten years ago, the CAT scan was just coming into existence. Ten years ago, my doctor had been in high school. I was a bit concerned about his experience. "Do you think I have a tumor?" I asked.

"Let's see what the myelogram shows before we start worrying." He sidestepped out of the room. "I'll see you tomorrow."

I looked at Len, unable to put into words everything I was thinking. "Honey, you should go home. I'll need some things brought to the hospital tomorrow." His face looked pinched, squeezed with concern. "Don't worry, I'll be fine."

After Len left, I stared out my window where boughs of tall evergreens framed the view of the distant hills. Dingy gray smog stained the cloudless June sky. I absently rubbed my abdomen, but I couldn't feel my own touch. In just a few hours, my condition had deteriorated. I couldn't wiggle a toe or move a leg. What was happening to me? I should have rushed to the doctor when I first noticed the weakness in my left leg. I should have realized something was wrong. My baby was due in less than six weeks. Worry and fear gnawed like hungry rats at the remnants of my optimism.

I hated to admit I was concerned about the myelogram. What would happen to my baby? Would the baby be affected by the radiation? I wondered how many pregnant women had undergone a myelogram. Leave it to me to be different—red skin, scoliosis, lopsided legs, and now paralysis. I should be thankful my first child would be born soon—and I was. But how could I mother from a wheelchair? People did. I knew that. Yet, it seemed an insurmountable task. Without family in the state, how would Len and I manage?

Early Friday morning, a porter whisked me to the radiology department for the dreaded myelogram. My advanced pregnant state and inability to move the lower half of my body surprised the technicians. They eased me onto a table as hard as concrete despite its flimsy pad and then turned me on my left side. Folding a lead apron around my chest and abdomen to protect the baby from radiation exposure, they positioned me with my knees pulled as tight toward my chest as my protruding abdomen allowed.

199

Dr. Larkin arrived in green scrubs, looking eager to begin. I wasn't sure I was ready. Fumes of Betadine wafted to my nostrils as the doctor prepped the area, and I heard the rustle of the paper drapes. The doctor anesthetized my back, performed the lumbar puncture, and then warned me when he started to inject the dye. I felt a surge of heat flow into my legs. Electric sparks shot down both legs, and one leg jerked like a frog's in a biology experiment. Quickly after the injection, I was tilted head down at a forty-five degree angle, gravity and the lead apron conspiring to push me off the table. Although sturdy shoulder restraints thwarted my downward progress, they ground painfully into my bones. With arms extended, I clenched my hands around small grips, yet my arms quivered in response to my weak counter pressure.

"How're you doing, Debbie?" Dr. Larkin asked.

"Oh, peachy!"

"Just hang on a little longer."

Easy for him to say. I clung to the table like a mountain climber on a steep face. My arms trembled. What was taking so long? I tried to distract myself and practice Lamaze breathing when it occurred to me that Len and I had not completed the course.

Dr. Larkin mumbled under his breath something wasn't quite right with the procedure. "Put her flat again," he said sharply.

The table hummed as it returned to the horizontal position.

"Debbie, the dye's supposed to move from the puncture site to your head when you're tilted down," Dr. Larkin said. "In your case, the dye hasn't moved at all."

"What's that mean?"

"Something's preventing the flow of the dye from moving through the subarachnoid space. You have a major block in your lumbar area, and I don't know what's causing it. I'd like to do a CAT scan but not while you're pregnant. I need to discuss some things with Dr. Alverez and decide on a course of action. For right now, stay flat in bed for eight hours, especially your head. Drinking plenty of fluids prevents headaches sometimes caused by the lumbar puncture. I'll check on you later."

Relieved of my lead weight, I inhaled a deep breath. My arms and shoulders ached from their ordeal, but I was grateful to have finished the procedure.

\*      \*      \*

# CHAPTER TWENTY-FOUR—MORE PROBLEMS

Dr. Alverez, my gynecologist for five years, arrived Saturday morning, shaking his head. Immaculate in his knee-length lab coat, tie knotted neatly at the collar of his crisp dress shirt, he stepped closer to my bed. His brown eyes skimmed over my unmoving bulk. "Debbie, Debbie, what is happening?"

I wished I knew. "Well, I suppose you've talked with Dr. Larkin."

"Yes, I spoke with him. I don't think the baby is causing your problem, but maybe the pregnancy is exacerbating it. I'd like to do an ultrasound to determine the size of the baby. If the baby is big enough, we may have to do a cesarean section. Dr. Larkin wants you delivered so you can undergo additional tests."

The doctor's soft-spoken words rolled off his tongue with the pleasant cadence indicative of his Latin heritage, calming me regardless of the words' impact. I studied my painted red fingernails. "Providing the baby is big enough, when would you do the C-section?"

"Probably on Monday afternoon."

"Tomorrow is Father's Day! Too bad Len won't be a father, yet."

He reached down and squeezed my hand. "We'll make a decision after I check your ultrasound."

Later, Dr. Larkin and Dr. Ladisky arrived simultaneously to assess my neurologic function (or deterioration). I succumbed to their pinpricks, tuning forks, and game of "Guess which toe I'm touching?"

"Dr. Alverez was here today," I told the doctors. "He ordered an ultrasound to determine the baby's size."

"Yes, I read his note." Dr. Larkin eyed my birthmark before he met my gaze. "I'd like to get the baby out as soon as possible, so I can do more tests. We should do another myelogram after delivery and a CAT scan at the very least. We just don't know what is causing the paralysis."

Dr. Ladisky nodded.

*Oh, no. Not another myelogram.*

Dr. Larkin continued, "I'm concerned you may have permanent damage if we do not diagnose and arrest the problem. You might never walk again."

"No! You're wrong! I know I will walk again. I'm a nurse. I have to walk . . . for my baby." Despite the bleak outlook offered by the doctor, I saw myself walking out of the hospital, my beautiful baby cradled in my arms. I did not accept that I would never walk again or pedal a bicycle or skip or jump or dance or push my baby in a stroller. My assertions quickly chased the doctors from the room.

The usual hospital routine consumed the day. The cold hot foods and hot cold foods came at irregularly scheduled times. My undiminished appetite kept Len running to the cafeteria for additional provisions to sustain my cravings: candy bars, popcorn, pie, and ice cream. Between trips, Len told me he had talked with our parents.

After twelve years on the road with the pictorial company, my in-laws had retired, settling in Texas near Len's oldest brother. Although they offered to come to California, Len had advised them to hold off.

Dad couldn't get away from a busy construction season, so Mom elected him to watch over my sister Diane, the recent high school graduate. Mom issued orders, worried, packed, and prepared to board the next plane whenever I needed her.

With my ultrasound completed, I didn't have any more tests scheduled, and Len and I danced around the more serious topics. "Maybe we should think of names for the baby," I said.

Len's eyes brightened as he stood beside me. "Okay."

"I like Laura for a girl. Or maybe, we could put both our names together for a new name, like Deben. Deben Renee," I practiced.

Len sank into the chair next to my bed. "No, I don't like that. I choose Christie—like Christie Brinkley." He grinned, exposing dental work that had closed the gap between his front teeth.

I shot him a look that said I knew he liked more besides the name of the famous model. "Christie is nice. What about a middle name?"

"Well . . ."

"How about Michelle?"

"Christie Michelle. Yeah, okay." He didn't sound enthused about Michelle. "Not Christine, just Christie with an *ie*. That way no one will shorten her name. You must have a girl. I really want a daughter."

"I know you do, but what if it's a boy?"

"You get to name him. I'll name the girl."

I thought for a moment. "How about Timothy? Timothy Something."

Len wrinkled his nose and pointed a finger at me. "You just better have a girl." He leaned over and embraced me. "I love you. You know I need you and so will our baby. You just concentrate on walking again."

I clung to him. "I love you, too. Don't worry. Someday we'll laugh about all this." I echoed one of his frequent expressions.

*     *     *

Dr. Larkin appeared early Sunday morning and conducted another exam. The bumps on my birthmark continued to fascinate him as if they held an answer to a puzzle. "I believe Dr. Alverez will be in to discuss your C-section. I am concerned about the anesthesia. As you know, we found a severe blockage somewhere in the lower thoracic/upper lumbar spine."

I visualized the spine—the upper cervical, the middle thoracic, and the lower lumbar areas.

He continued, "The myelogram dye did not move at all beyond the injection site which means you cannot receive a spinal block. I will inform Dr. Alverez of this."

"Oh good," I muttered. He gave me a wry smile on his way out.

Dr. Alverez confirmed I was scheduled for a C-section on Monday. "I understand that due to your back problem, spinal anesthesia is impossible."

"So I heard."

He placed one hand on the bed rail and took a deep breath. "We'll have to do the section under general anesthetic. This is not at all good for the baby because the baby receives what you do and will be sleepy, too. We must quickly deliver the baby before it receives too much anesthesia."

I nodded. "Will Len be permitted in the delivery room?" I knew hospital policy banned family from the delivery room during general anesthesia cases, but I hoped the doctor would make an exception.

Dr. Alverez frowned. "It is not a pleasant sight to see your wife intubated and unresponsive."

"Oh, Len's heard many of my gory tales over the years, so I don't think that will bother him."

Dr. Alverez chuckled. "Then it won't be a problem. We'll do the section around one or two. Do you have a pediatrician lined up?"

"Gosh, we were in the process of choosing one before I landed in here. Will you contact Dr. Kaufman for me?"

"Yes. He must be in attendance for C-sections."

"I realize that and would appreciate him accepting."

"Good. Is there anything else I can do for you?"

"Not right now. I can't believe tomorrow I'll be a mom. Everything's happening so fast, I'm a little overwhelmed."

Dr. Alverez patted my hand, his expression somber. "You have a right to be." A smile slowly formed on his lips. "I must tell you I will be leaving for three weeks following your delivery."

"What?"

His smile grew wider. "I'm getting married. Dr. Barrett, an associate, will assist me in the C-section, and he will follow your care afterwards."

"I guess I'm lucky you were still here for this event."

"Everything will be done to get you back to normal."

I hoped he was right.

*        *        *

A familiar husky voice woke me the morning of my child's birthday, June 20, 1983. "Good morning Debbie."

I struggled awake, remembering I had been transferred to the labor and delivery department the night before. "Hi, there."

Tina, one of the maternity nurses, smiled and busied herself arranging equipment on the bedside table. "I have to start an IV on you."

"Okay, I know you're the expert. But I understand you use very large needles here."

She snickered. "Nothing but the best." With expert ability, Tina inserted a large-bore IV cannula into a plump vein in my forearm and started the dextrose solution. "I also need to put in a Foley catheter."

"Oh, joy!" Getting me into the proper position for the insertion of the urinary catheter was a comical endeavor. I had trouble controlling where my legs should stay during the procedure. They kept collapsing inward, hindering Tina from accomplishing her task. My giggling amplified the problem.

"Look, if you don't behave, I'll have to tie your knees to the side rails," Tina said.

I giggled again. Ultimately, Tina succeeded in placing the catheter.

A short time later, I noticed a dark, rusty-red color to the urine in my catheter tube. I rang for the nurse. While she checked my vital signs, I told her I had taken a Percodan pain pill last evening. Percodan contained aspirin and could activate bleeding, but I didn't know how the drug would affect a pregnant patient or one in my unusual condition.

When Dr. Ingram marched slowly into my room, careful not to displace a lock of his slick, razor-cut hair, I feared trouble. His erect posture, meticulous appearance, and aloof demeanor buffered his specialty—oncology and hematology. "I'm Dr. Ingram, a hematologist. Dr. Alverez asked that I see you because of the blood in your urine." He peeked at the red urine in my catheter tube. "You had a Percodan yesterday?"

I finally found my ability to speak. "Yes, I did."

He didn't look at me. "Have you ever had bleeding problems in the past?"

"A cut on my birthmark takes longer to clot."

"I see." He collected a history from me, remaining dispassionate, almost distracted. "You are having surgery this afternoon, and a prolonged bleeding time could be very dangerous. I'm going to order some blood tests, a clotting time, and a urinalysis. You may have some renal involvement which should probably be checked out by a nephrologist at some point in time. I'll order the tests and see where we go from there." His solemn expression intact, he left without a whisper of a breeze.

*What next?* I had to give myself a pep talk or I'd succumb to the "Why me?" syndrome. I soon would be a mom, and that thought sustained me. I imagined what the baby would look like, if it would be a boy or girl, how Len would do during the delivery, how I would feel afterwards.

A laboratory technician called my name, interrupting my speculations. "It's time for blood tests." After the blood was drawn, the tech performed a clotting time. Normal clotting time is between five and seven minutes; however, mine was prolonged, which increased the risk of hemorrhage during surgery.

Dr. Ingram returned briefly to give me the test results. "You have thrombocytopenia, a low platelet count. I'm ordering twenty units of platelets to be administered as soon as possible. Afterwards, we'll get a repeat test."

Thrombocytopenia could be caused by tumors, drug toxicity, or infection. Without an adequate platelet count, surgery would be delayed. I tried not to think of the causes, consequences, or complications of the low platelet count. I prayed to God for strength to overcome each and every obstacle that lay ahead. I prayed for God to protect my child and ensure a safe delivery into the world. I prayed to know my child.

The morning hours slipped by. I received my twenty units of platelets and waited for word of my pending surgery.

Dr. Wiest, a youthful anesthesiologist, introduced himself. He reported my repeat platelet count was normal; therefore, surgery would proceed. "I know about your back problem."

"Please don't give me too much anesthesia. I want to wake up quickly to see my baby."

"This is a light anesthesia," he explained. "You'll be awake before you get to the recovery room."

"Good. Of course, I don't want to feel Dr. Alverez sewing me closed."

"Don't worry about that."

"Is it okay for my husband to be in the room?"

"I think that will be fine. But if he feels the need for air or whatever, he can easily leave."

I smiled. "I understand."

"See you soon then."

When Len arrived, I told him the parade of doctors had grown and explained what had transpired that morning. He cracked a few jokes, his way to lighten a serious situation. Sitting on the corner of my bed, he held my hand and stroked my arm, but neither of us acknowledged the palpable tension squeezing our hearts.

Before long, one of the nurses came to escort Len to a changing room. Len wished me good luck and kissed me. "Remember you must have a girl, or we'll just put it back."

Finally, splayed beneath a large silver spotlight in the delivery suite, I watched the room fill with people, each attending to their specific job. Dr. Wiest attached the EKG electrodes to my chest, fitted a blood pressure cuff around one arm, and tied the arm with the IV to a board jutting out from the table. Someone bathed my abdomen with Betadine in preparation for the surgical incision.

The scrub nurse surprised me when she said hello. I knew Miriam, the operating room instructor, when I worked in the Nursing Education Department. The nursery nurse, also a previous Nursing Ed coworker, prepared to receive the baby. Overseeing the entire production, the head nurse of the labor and delivery unit stood by with our camera ready. I felt secure and calm, surrounded by such qualified nurses.

When Len rustled into the room in his royal-blue, paper scrubs, looking like a blue bird on his solo flight, I had to smile. He acted self-conscious in his costume and mask. I warned him not to faint on the doctors or me. That seemed to relax him a bit although his blue eyes darted over the foreign landscape as if searching for a place to hide.

Like an orchestra conductor, Dr. Alverez entered the delivery suite exuding confidence. He knew everyone had done his or her job preparing for his performance. While he gowned and gloved, he offered me a few encouraging words. With all eyes upon him, Dr. Alverez assumed his position at my side. He directed Len to stand behind the drape near my head while he made the incision. Afterwards, Len could move closer. I glimpsed the steel scalpel like a baton in the doctor's raised hand. He reminded the anesthesiologist the baby had to be delivered as quickly as possible after the induction of anesthesia. Holding the scalpel poised over my abdomen, Dr. Alverez asked Dr. Wiest, "Is she out yet?"

*Don't let him cut me before I'm asleep.* I never heard the reply.

*   *   *

# CHAPTER TWENTY-FIVE—SEPARATION ANXIETY

A feeling of motion pulled me back to reality. I heard my name and swam through the riptide as the anesthetic relinquished its grip on my mind. I opened my eyes and squinted. There was Len. The C-section must be over.

Len, grinning as if he'd won the lottery, hustled alongside the rolling gurney. "We have a beautiful baby daughter. You did a good job."

My mouth felt as if someone left a dirty sock in it. I pried my lips apart. "What does she look like?"

"She's absolutely perfect. She has a lot of really dark hair, and she cries good."

"Oh, I'm so glad you got your girl. I can't wait to see her."

Len grasped my hand. "You have to go to recovery first. They've already taken the baby to the nursery. I'll go see her while they tend to you."

I smiled. "Okay."

"Then I have to make my phone calls." Len kissed my hand. "Be back shortly."

In the recovery room, I drifted on waves of sleep. Hands reached beneath my blankets to explore, palpate, pain, and soothe. I fought the undertow and eventually surfaced in a private room on the postpartum unit. Nurses slid a board under me and slid me into bed. Thigh-length stockings clung like a wet suit to my paralyzed legs.

Voices intruded into my consciousness. I was unaware of time and, oddly, felt no pain. Sensing a presence, I shook off my lethargy and recognized Len. "When can I see the baby?" I asked in a raspy voice.

Len brushed a stray lock of hair from my forehead. "The baby's still in the nursery. She's a little small, so they put her in an incubator."

I clutched his hand. "How much did she weigh?"

"Five pounds six ounces. And she's eighteen inches long." He spoke with a note of pride. "I already told them her name is Christie. She was born at 1:38 p.m." Len looked out the window, then at me. "That Dr. Alverez is one hell of a surgeon. He delivered the baby *thirty seconds* after you were put under. It was so fast." Len rattled the bed rail. "He jiggled the table, and water gushed all over the place. Dr. Alverez slid his arm inside you, and, seconds later, he pulled out the baby. When he said, 'It's a girl,' I got tears in my eyes." Len rubbed a hand over his face. "Then Dr. Alverez told me to come closer, and he handed me the scissors and told me to cut the cord. I was nervous, but I did it. The baby was crying and wiggling. Her hair is dark like yours was in your baby pictures."

Tears sprang to my eyes. "Did you hold her yet?"

"After the cord was cut, the nurse put her on a warming tray and put drops in her eyes and sucked junk out of her nose."

"That's called suctioning and it's mucous."

"Okay. The baby doctor . . ."

"Dr. Kaufman," I said.

". . . examined her, doing his doctor thing. He said she had all the necessary parts in all the correct places. Then the nurse wrapped her in a blanket and placed her in my arms." His eyes closed for a moment. "She is so tiny and beautiful. While you were getting sewed up, I posed for pictures." Len's happiness lighted the room and my heart.

"When can I see her?" Now that I was coherent, I wanted to hold my daughter.

Len sat down in a chair next to the bed and peered between the side rails at me. "I saw the baby in the nursery after her bath. She wasn't red and wrinkled like some babies. She was a normal pink—the prettiest in the world!"

"When can I see her?"

Len gazed past me. "Dr. Kaufman has been with her off and on and won't let her out of the incubator, yet. He said he'd be in to talk to you."

"You're scaring me. Is she okay?"

Len nodded. "Yes, dear, she's fine. They need to keep her warm."

I whispered a quick prayer that God would protect my child. "Did you call everyone?"

"Sure did. Everyone was happy but concerned for you, too. How do you feel, by the way?"

"Fine, I guess. I don't hurt very much, and I still can't move my legs. Maybe that's a blessing."

"Now you need to get better. You have a new daughter to take care of."

"I know."

While the hours passed, I ate a light dinner, then dozed. Len volleyed between the nursery and me, assuring me Christie was doing fine.

A young, disheveled doctor hurried into my room. "I'm Dr. Kaufman," he sighed and shook my hand. "I've been watching the baby—Christie—all day. She's had breathing difficulties, not uncommon in premature babies." I held my breath. "Her Apgars were ten and nine, not bad." I exhaled. "She also had some retractions, indicating mild respiratory distress. I don't think she's in any danger, but we may need to transfer her to another facility equipped with an NICU (neonatal intensive care unit). I'll be around for a while to watch her, and I'll keep you posted." He rushed out.

The doctor's report and hasty departure frightened me. No wonder I hadn't been able to hold my daughter.

Len bowed his head, then looked at me. "It's going to be okay."

"I know."

The evening hours inched along while we waited for word of Christie's condition. I wanted to get up and walk down the hall to the nursery and see for myself what was happening. But that was impossible. I couldn't even take care of myself.

Ann, a nursery nurse, came to my room with a Polaroid photograph of my daughter. Ann claimed the picture wasn't too great, but she thought it might comfort me. I strained to see the details in the fuzzy picture, but I couldn't make out much more than a tiny blanketed form inside an Isolette. I clung to the picture and waited for the doctor to give his report.

Shortly before ten o'clock, Dr. Kaufman told us he planned to transfer Christie to an NICU. "Just to be on the safe side," he assured us. "She doesn't seem to be in any trouble now, but if there should be a change during the night, I'd like her to be in a place where they could properly treat her. This is just a precautionary measure," he reaffirmed.

Len and I nodded our consent. Dr. Kaufman's assurance did not alleviate my anxiety. I knew what could happen. I felt guilty. My baby was delivered prematurely because of my problems. Now, she had to fight because I failed her.

Len told me the transport team had arrived to take Christie to the other hospital. I held my Polaroid picture as tears threatened. Suddenly, the team wheeled an Isolette into my room. I could hardly contain my surprise. Although Christie was all bundled for her trip, the nurse opened the Isolette, lifted out the baby, and presented her to me.

My tiny daughter felt wonderful in my arms. Len drew close, so we could examine our child and delight over every feature. Christie had Len's thick eyebrows, but my pug nose sat like a rosebud on her angelic face. She blinked open her blue-gray eyes; her thick, long lashes looked coated with mascara. Above her small ears, Christie's dark, almost-black hair felt like silk. Her upturned mouth fluttered when I kissed her fuzzy cheek. I prayed for God to watch over her.

Tears moistened my eyes. "She's absolutely gorgeous!"

Len grinned. "She certainly is."

"I can't believe she's so perfect." I wanted to unwrap my gift, examine every inch of her, but the nurse indicated it was time for them to leave. Reluctantly, I relinquished my child. "Bye, sweetheart. Hurry back to Mommy."

Len and I hugged tightly, silently drawing strength from each other. "Remember, the doctor said this was just a precaution," he reminded me.

"I know. You better get going."

"Yes, they told me I have to sign some admitting paperwork for Christie. After I see that she's settled, I'll head home."

"You get some rest. Don't worry about me. Are you going to see the baby tomorrow?"

"You bet! Afterwards I'll come by to see you and give you a full report." He saluted, then kissed me good-bye, somehow finding the energy to hurry out the door.

\*      \*      \*

Less than twenty-four hours later, I returned to radiology for a myelogram encore. Fortunately, this time, I received sedation to help me through the procedure. As predicted, Dr. Larkin seemed anxious to get down to business. No rest for a new mother.

Dr. Larkin again injected the dye, and I was assisted onto my abdomen. Straps secured my ankles to the table. When the table tilted to lift my feet skyward, I felt like a snared marlin, dangled from a hook above the dock, waiting for the fisherman to pose for a photograph. The position would have been intolerable so soon after abdominal surgery, but my decreased sensation served some advantage. Straining to prevent a headlong slide to the floor made my arms quiver, and surging blood pounded a rhythm in my head. Like the last time, Dr. Larkin grumbled under his breath, clearly unsatisfied with the dye's progress. It just wouldn't move.

Suddenly, Dr. Larkin wanted me to sit up. He explained his intention to inject the dye into the cervical area of the spine, then take x-rays as the dye flowed down toward my lower lumbar spine. I had no idea this was a possible alternative. While seated, my right neck and shoulder area were prepped and draped for the puncture. When Dr. Larkin inserted the needle, a piercing pain shot through my head. I felt the needle tunneling inward as if penetrating my brain. My watery eyes overflowed when he injected the dye. My head pounded in pain.

The fluoroscopy revealed another blockage in the upper thoracic area. Dr. Larkin seemed baffled by this new revelation. Finally, he terminated the exam. "I don't know why the dye won't move," he said. "I think I'll order a CAT scan to see what that shows." He threw his gloves on the used Mayo stand. "I'll see you later."

The pain in my head waned as I rode the gurney back to my room on the fifth floor. Once I was settled in bed, the parade of doctors commenced.

Dr. Alverez examined my incision before turning me over to the care of his associate. He wanted to see me in six weeks for a follow-up. "I want to see you walk into the office."

"I will. I hope you have a wonderful wedding and honeymoon. Thank you for everything you've done and for my beautiful baby daughter."

He shook my hand. "You are a very special person, Debbie."

Next, my neurologist appeared, laughing. "I couldn't find the postpartum unit." Another neuro exam revealed little change for better or worse. We agreed to start physical therapy on my legs to strengthen the muscles.

"Sounds like work," I said.

"Can't have you getting too lazy," Dr. Ladisky said. "I'll write the orders and see you tomorrow."

Dr. Wiest, the anesthesiologist, visited briefly to determine my recovery from the anesthesia. I thanked him for the light sleep and told him I felt fine, no hangover.

My internist, Dr. Roland, surprised me with a visit. He heard of my admission through the hospital grapevine and offered to be available for anything I needed.

I explained what I knew thus far and Dr. Larkin's plans for a CAT scan. "Right now, I guess, no one knows too much."

"Dr. Larkin will have an answer for your paralysis soon, I'm sure," Dr. Roland said.

"I hope so."

Dr. Kaufman completed the parade. He had seen Christie at the other hospital and reported she was doing fine. ". . . one of the healthiest in the NICU."

"When will she be discharged?"

"We'll watch her a couple more days, see how she's eating. Respiratory function's okay, no problems." Dr. Kaufman smiled. "Are you planning on breast feeding?"

"Yes, I hope to."

"We'll try her on a formula similar to breast milk for her first feedings. The transition should be easy."

"Good."

*       *       *

The early evening hours proved to be equally busy. I occupied my time talking on the phone, chatting with the nurses, and pumping my breasts. Freshly scrubbed and primped, I dined alone, waiting for Len. When at last he arrived, I couldn't wait to hear every detail from his visit with our daughter.

His words tumbled out as if he couldn't wait to tell me about his experience. "I had to scrub, mask, and gown like a doctor. When I got inside the unit, there was Christie in that little closed-in crib."

"Isolette," I said, smiling.

"They disconnected some of her wires and wrapped her up all snug in a blanket and put her in my arms." His eyes sparkled with joy. "They even had a rocking chair for me next to the Isolette. She was so good and quiet, just beautiful."

I wished I could have seen that. "So, how is she?"

"Just fine. In fact, everyone wondered why she was there because she's so healthy. You should see how sick some of those poor babies are. We're lucky our baby doesn't have such problems."

"We sure are."

*　　　*　　　*

# CHAPTER TWENTY-SIX—WHAT NEXT?

My second day of motherhood, Wednesday, June 22, started with morning care and breast pumping, then breakfast, a bed bath, and doctors' rounds. Cathy, a tall physical therapist, arrived to evaluate my strengths—or rather my weaknesses. She found my legs as flaccid as cooked spaghetti and frowned.

"Is something wrong?" I asked.

She shook her head. "Oh no, not at all. I just don't get many orders to do therapy on the postpartum unit. I haven't read your chart yet, so forgive my confusion."

"I'm sure the nurses on this unit are confused, too. I'm not their typical patient." I gave Cathy an abbreviated version of my hospitalization while she put my legs through a series of motions.

"Wow!" She continued exercising my legs. "I can't believe it. Do they know what's causing the paralysis?"

"Not yet. I'm still having tests. I think the CAT scan is later today."

When the porter came to take me for the CAT scan, he maneuvered my wheelchair out of the hospital toward a trailer housing the portable scanner. During the three-minute ride to the trailer, sunshine poured over me, so I yanked up my sleeves. "Maybe I can get a suntan. I should have an outing like this every day." The porter ignored the warm sun, chirping birds, and me.

After reviewing the CAT scan, Dr. Larkin reported the results were unclear. "I see a mass on the films, but I want to do another test to be certain of a diagnosis."

I slapped my hands against the mattress. "Now what?"

"Spinal angios." He delved into an explanation.

"Spinal angios?" I whispered, not listening to his description of the procedure.

As a nurse, I had instructed patients about the test, but I never dreamed I'd be on the receiving end.

Dr. Larkin broke into my wandering thoughts. "Any questions?"

"When?"

"I'll try to get you on the schedule tomorrow." He began the neuro exam. "Have you felt any different since your delivery?"

"No better, no worse. I started P.T. today. Gotta keep my muscles strong."

Dr. Larkin smiled. "Good, good."

My evening visit with Len focused on Christie and her progress. He described holding her and raved about her beauty. I folded my empty arms across my chest.

"I took Rob with me today," Len said.

"Oh, that was nice."

"With all her wires and lines, he was afraid to hold her, but he got a good look."

"I'm sure you were proud to show off your daughter."

"Bonding," Len announced. "That's what the nurses say I'm doing—bonding."

My heart knotted. "I'm glad one of us can do that." But knowing my husband had the support of our friend, Rob, comforted me.

Len soon left for home. Talk of bonding reminded me of the past. Thanks to Rob, Len and I ended up in California.

*     *     *

The guys—Len and his comic friend, Rob, from college—wanted to try their luck in Hollywood. So in the spring of 1977, Len and I put the mobile home, boat, and sports car up for sale. By August, we had sold our possessions and set a departure date for September 4. Carol, a girl on my bowling team who happened to be dating Rob, decided to travel west with us and then move to Arizona, where her mom lived. I gave my notice at the hospital, and the countdown was on.

The four of us rented a U-Haul trailer large enough for our personal and household possessions. Len and Rob worked hard packing the cargo, but our barbeque grill didn't fit and had to be left behind with a neighbor. When Len attached the U-Haul to our Pontiac Bonneville, the back of the car sagged to the ground. The load outweighed the twenty-three-foot, fly-bridge, cabin cruiser that the car had towed with ease. Muttering under his breath, Len took the car to have the hitch reinforced.

The delay made parting more intense. Grandma wailed that she'd never see us. Grandpa stalked back and forth across the lawn, puffing his pipe and grumbling in German. Mom and I hugged and hugged, crying buckets and making all sorts of promises. With a somber expression, Dad shook his head. "Be careful," he said. I embraced my brother and sister. Roger would soon be entering his junior year at the University of Missouri, and Diane was beginning eighth grade. How could I leave?

Suddenly, I had second thoughts. I didn't know where I would be living, didn't have a job, and didn't know a soul in California. I must be nuts! My life was wonderful, balanced, and sane. I should have thought this out better for now it was too late to reconsider. My home was sold. My boat was sold. Len's car was sold. And the barbeque donated to the neighbor.

Before I could bail out, Len returned with the car's reinforced trailer hitch, and I said my good-byes amid tears and pained smiles and climbed into the car. As the horizon of the western plain swallowed up the hot September sun, I held our dog Bubbles and waved farewell.

For nearly a month, the four of us traveled more than two thousand miles, camping our way west like pioneers. Rob and Carol trailed the U-Haul in Carol's convertible with Ali, Rob's boxer, planted in the backseat, tongue flapping in the wind. South of Santa Barbara, California, Len and I became separated from Rob and Carol. When Len and I reached Los Angeles at the end of September, we placed an ad in the newspaper to locate them. Several days later, we reunited.

The long trip wasn't without its trials. We disagreed, argued, and even parted company for three days, but we formed close friendships. Carol left for Arizona while Rob, Len, and I settled into respective apartments and tried to adjust to Hollywood. With bonds made stronger on our trip, I knew I could count on Rob . . . always.

*     *     *

I reached for the electric breast pump and sighed. Bonding! This wasn't how I pictured my bonding experience.

Every June 23, Len and I celebrated "Our Day," the day we met in 1968. In celebration of that fifteen-year anniversary, today was "enema day." Adding to my misery, the angiogram procedure put my breakfast on hold.

Angiography is x-ray visualization of blood vessels to determine the presence of a blockage. After introducing a catheter into the femoral artery, located in the groin, dye is injected and x-rays follow. I tried to calm my jitters, but the room's frigid temperature contributed to my angst. I tolerated the procedure until the dye injection, and then I felt as if my legs were on fire and there wasn't a fireman around.

Dr. Larkin discussed the results of the angiogram with me the next morning. He explained I had a blockage from the upper thoracic spine to the lower lumbar spine—most of my back.

I swallowed the lump in my throat. "Do you know what's causing it?"

"It could be a tumor." He glanced at my arm. "Or something related to your birthmark. I think we should do exploratory surgery to examine the area and take a biopsy."

"Surgery! Are you sure?"

"I'm not certain," he admitted. "I've discussed your case with the radiation doctors in the event it's necessary to radiate the growth. Without surgery, I can't be sure of what we're dealing with."

"I see." I paused. "I think I'd like another consult." The words shot from my mouth, surprising me. "I'd like a second opinion before I make any decision about surgery."

Dr. Larkin wasn't smiling. "I agree. That's a good idea. I'll notify Dr. Wilson to see you as soon as possible. And also, one of the radiation doctors." He departed.

*Not surgery! I can't go through that again.*

Before I had time to mull over my problem, Dr. Kaufman arrived, a wide smile on his narrow face. Like catching measles, I broke out in a smile, too. "What are you so happy about?"

He grinned. "I have good news. I discharged Christie from NICU today."

"That's wonderful! When will she arrive?"

"Later this afternoon," he said. "We couldn't keep such a healthy baby in NICU any longer. She's eating, and her respiratory function's fine."

"I'm so thankful." Quickly I telephoned Len to tell him about Christie and about Dr. Larkin's news.

"I'll be up this afternoon," Len said. "Your mom comes in tonight, so I have to go to the airport."

I almost forgot about Mom's arrival. Was it Friday already? I had been here one week and didn't know much more now than I did when I was admitted. Thank goodness Mom would be here. For a while, I could lean on her.

By noon, I had seen my pack of doctors and heard their differing opinions. Sometime after my tasteless lunch, Dr. Braddock introduced himself as a specialist in the field of radiation. He asserted that the benefit of radiation in combination with physical therapy could alleviate my problems. He warned me of the side effects of radiation—anorexia, nausea, vomiting, headaches, diarrhea, and lethargy. Long-term effects could include disturbances to blood cell formation or cancer.

"I suggest you have the surgery Dr. Larkin proposes," Dr. Braddock said. "I would like to know specifically where to radiate; that is, if you agree to the treatment."

"Would you know where to radiate without my having the surgery?"

"Knowing the specific area, we can minimize the amount of radiation you receive. Otherwise, we would have to radiate a larger section, increasing your exposure which may cause side effects or damage to the spinal cord," he explained.

"I understand, but I'm not able to make a decision, yet. I'm getting a second consult today from Dr. Wilson. Maybe after I speak with him, I can decide."

"You should obtain all the information you can. I'll check back with you after you've had some time to think.

I'm available if you have any questions." He excused himself.

Soon, I was honored by one of the great doctor gods of the hospital, Dr. Wilson. His mere presence frightened most of the staff. Familiar with his reputation, I had little contact with him beyond a few telephone conversations. He was king of neurosurgery at St. Joe's, a master surgeon who demanded perfection from those participating in his patients' care. Attired in a starched, white lab coat, his name and specialty embroidered above his breast pocket, the "god" entered my room and promptly settled into the rocking chair across from my bed.

"I am Dr. Wilson," he proclaimed.

I would have risen if I was able. "Nice to meet you, Dr. Wilson."

"Dr. Larkin asked me to see you for a second opinion." He crossed his legs and rested his elbows on the chair arms. "I've reviewed your films and history." He looked at my covered legs. "I suppose you want to know if you should have surgery?"

"Well, I'm confused. Dr. Larkin isn't sure what's causing my problem and feels surgery is necessary to determine the cause and extent of the problem. At least, that's my interpretation of his explanation."

His eyes momentarily searched the ceiling. "It's really very simple. Your cord compression is caused by your birthmark." He tilted his head to one side, inspecting his trousers, and tweaked the razor crease. "During pregnancy, blood volume increases to provide nourishment to the developing fetus. Blood vessels dilate. Your birthmark, being a vascular malformation, is not only external but internal as well. In your case, it's wrapped around your spinal cord. As the blood vessels dilate, they press on the cord, interrupting the impulses from your brain to your legs. Your diminished sensation is due to that compression. The treatment of choice is to radiate the overgrowth of blood vessels; in other words, shrink them, so they won't compress the cord. You don't need surgery," he declared.

I folded my hands together. "Dr. Braddock told me surgery would define the area needing radiation."

"I'm not so sure it's necessary. I've seen cases like this and feel only radiation is needed." He nodded, pushed himself up from the chair, and departed on an invisible red carpet.

The "god" hath spoken. He was certain I didn't need surgery. It made sense, but I didn't want more radiation than necessary. Maybe I did need the surgery to define the area. I was more confused than ever.

When Dr. Larkin made an appearance, I blasted him with both barrels. "I saw Dr. Wilson."

"Good, good," he said with a smug smile.

"He said surgery is unnecessary. My birthmark is the cause of my cord compression, and radiation would alleviate the problem.

His smile faded. "I'm sure Dr. Wilson knows what he is saying." He fidgeted. "You realize none of the tests indicate the depth or exact location of the mass?"

"So I might get too much radiation in order to remedy the problem?"

He nodded. "That certainly is a concern. I feel surgery is needed for a definitive diagnosis and treatment plan."

"I don't know what to do. Everyone has a different opinion." I pulled myself into a more upright position. "I want a conference. I want ALL my doctors together in this room to discuss the pros and cons. Do you even read each other's notes?"

"Okay," Dr. Larkin said, his grin reappearing. "I'll arrange a meeting of the minds, say Monday morning?"

"That's fine."

I sighed and flopped back onto the pillows. I'd wait until after the powwow on Monday to make a decision. Besides, I had better things to do—like mothering my daughter. Thoughts of Christie chased away my turmoil.

\*　　\*　　\*

# CHAPTER TWENTY-SEVEN—REUNION

Four days after my C-section, I finally cradled my daughter in my arms and prepared to nurse her for the first time. Wearing a mustard-striped, knit cap, Christie wriggled and rooted before settling down to business. I inhaled her Baby Magic scent and thanked God for blessing me with such a beautiful child. When I gazed upon her, I forgot I couldn't walk and forgot about doctors and decisions.

Christie finished nursing and burped like a sailor. I fumbled with her blankets, eager to unwrap my gift. "Mommy wants to see what's underneath." Lanugo, a fine downy hair common in premies, covered her flawless skin. No birthmarks marred her. Miniature nails capped the tiny toes and fingers of her scrawny legs and arms. She flailed and stretched against the cool air. I hastily secured the blankets, but I couldn't resist a peek at her hair. I peeled off her stocking cap. "Oh, my goodness! They shaved half your head!"

A faint bruise colored the bald side of her head. I stroked her remaining locks, tears burning my eyes, and felt as if I had failed her. "I'm sorry you had to have an IV." I slipped the cap back on her head, and she drifted to sleep in my arms.

The nurse returned to take the baby to the nursery. "She's on demand feedings. We'll bring her to you when she's hungry, about every three hours. If you want to have her sooner, just let us know."

When Len appeared around dinner time, I was jotting notes in Christie's baby book. He moved with a springy step to my bedside. "I thought you'd be depressed after seeing the new doctors."

I waved a hand in the air. "Oh, forget about them. I got to feed Christie for the first time."

"She's back?"

"Yes! And it was wonderful to finally feed her. She knew just what to do."

"Wow! That's great! How's everything else with her?"

"She's perfect. I didn't notice any breathing problems, but they shaved her head."

"What?"

I pointed to my right temple. "Well, not her whole head, just one side, where they put the IV."

Len disappeared to steal a glimpse of Christie through the nursery window. Afterwards, we dined on steak, the traditional dinner usually served to new parents the night before mom's discharge. Although I wasn't going home, the nurses had ordered the meal to celebrate Christie's return. Following dinner, Len watched me nurse the baby. A look of tenderness, love, and happiness sparkled in his eyes. The serenity of the family moment banished my worries.

Len glanced at the wall clock. "I've got to get going. Your mom's plane will be in soon. Do you think she'll want to come to the hospital right away?"

I giggled. "I don't think the National Guard could keep her from her first grandchild. I'll tell the nurses to expect a late visitor."

His lips skimmed mine, and he dashed out the door.

I simmered like a teapot ready to whistle, waiting for Len to return with Mom. When at last she arrived, we hugged and cried. She seemed surprised and relieved to see I didn't look too terrible.

I wiped away my tears. "Are you tired?"

Mom sniffed. "Not really. I think I'm running on excitement."

"Would you like to meet your granddaughter?"

She clapped her hands together. "I can't wait."

The nurse made Mom scrub, then dress in a clean gown to receive Christie. Mom's blue eyes watered as she scrutinized her sleeping grandchild. "She's so small."

"She's grown some," Len said and stood a little straighter.

I thought Mom would faint from happiness, and for once she was quiet as she studied Christie.

"Well . . ." I coaxed.

"She's absolutely gorgeous. You both did a good job."

I smiled. "We think so, too. Sit down."

Mom lowered herself to the rocking chair, grasping Christie as if she had never before held a baby. "Well, I'm not prejudiced, but she's the most beautiful baby I've ever seen, next to her mommy, of course."

I laughed. "Like mother, like daughter."

*    *    *

On Sunday, Dr. Kaufman showed up on crutches, having sprained his ankle playing softball. He was pleased with Christie's progress, and reported that when she weighed six pounds, he'd send her home, maybe by the end of the week. I wondered if I'd be ready to leave.

Monday morning, the tribe of doctors gathered in my room for the powwow. Dr. Larkin started the discussion and voiced Dr. Wilson's view in his absence. Operate or just radiate? The medical men discussed the pros and cons. When all had been hashed and rehashed, the consensus was for surgery.

I dreaded surgery but feared that large doses of radiation would have severe side effects and cause me more harm. With little choice, I forced a smile. "Okay, you've convinced me."

Dr. Larkin almost smiled. "I'll have you scheduled for tomorrow."

When Dr. Ladisky suggested starting Decadron, a steroid, Dr. Larkin agreed.

I held up my hands. "Hold the phone. I'm breast-feeding my baby."

The doctors quieted, and then Dr. Larkin softly said, "Your body, including your hormones, needs to return to a normal state. The drug, while beneficial to you, could be passed to the baby in the breast milk. It would be best if you stopped."

The other doctors murmured among themselves.

I should stop breast-feeding after only two and a half days? Forced to look to the future, I rationalized that I needed to walk for my daughter's sake. To restore function to my legs, I would have to sacrifice breast-feeding. Well, bottle feeding did have certain advantages—Len could help with Christie's feedings.

I groaned as another obstacle hindered my mothering. "Okay, no breast-feeding. When will you start the Decadron?"

"As soon as possible so you'll receive several doses before surgery," Dr. Larkin said. "I'll have your OB order medication to dry up your milk."

I rolled my eyes. "Thanks for thinking of that."

"I'll be back in a minute." Dr. Larkin left, and the tribe filed out behind him.

I exhaled a long sigh. I didn't want surgery, but I wanted to know for certain what was happening inside me. Was it my birthmark or a tumor?

A sober Dr. Larkin returned. "I have to explain a few details about the surgery. First, I don't know what I'll find when I open you up, so I've arranged for a post-op bed in the intensive care unit."

My mouth went dry. "ICU?"

"Just in case," he said. "Second, the area could hemorrhage, so I'll have you typed and cross-matched for six units of blood." He cleared his throat. "Finally, the surgery could leave you paralyzed, comatose, or dead."

"Well, count me in."

He suppressed a smile and continued. "When I get a look at what's around your cord, it's possible I'll do nothing. If the paralysis is caused by your birthmark, the area may be too vascular to excise safely. Noting the location, I'll close, and you'll be brought back to this room."

"And then?"

"You'll start radiation and intense physical therapy, and we'll continue with the Decadron post-op. Decadron can cause side effects, as I'm sure you're aware."

"Yes—moon face, hump back, GI problems, hyperglycemia, infections, and a hairy body, to name a few."

He grinned. "I know. The first several doses will be pretty hefty, but I don't anticipate any problems. Do you have any questions?"

"Can I go home now? Seriously, what time is the big event?"

"Late morning. Don't eat or drink anything after midnight." He turned to go.

"One more thing . . ." I said, and he pivoted. ". . . I would like to choose my anesthesiologist. Do you prefer to work with any particular one?"

"I'm too new here to have any preferences."

I gave Dr. Larkin my first three choices, selected for their experience and proficiency.

"Okay, I'll arrange that. See you tomorrow." He left with my bulging chart.

I couldn't believe I was having surgery. Dr. Larkin seemed happy, but I felt a little like Frankenstein. I hoped I wouldn't need that ICU bed.

Periods spent bottle-feeding and holding Christie cheered me. I tried not to think about the upcoming surgery, but concerns popped uninvited into my head. One minute I was sure I'd made the correct choice, the next I was positive I'd made the biggest blunder of my life. Through trained eyes, I envisioned the worst scenarios described by Dr. Larkin. I didn't want to live with paralysis, so I had to trust that I'd made the correct decision. My fate rested in the hands of a rookie doctor and the good Lord.

When Dr. Green hustled into my room, relief at seeing my first choice of anesthesiologists softened my anxiety. The big man, seasoned with experience, shook my hand. "I understand you're having surgery tomorrow."

I smiled at his tan face and intense, dark eyes. "Yes, Dr. Larkin's going exploring."

He bowed his head toward me, then quietly explained the details of my upcoming anesthesia. His thorough

241

research of my case showed. He knew more about me than I did.

Mom and Len arrived after dinner, and I told them I had agreed to the surgery. I think they had sensed I was leaning toward that choice all along.

Doting on Christie distracted me. Mom's face glowed like a neon sign as she fed Christie her bottle. With the baby dozing in her arms, all peaceful, Mom yawned, and Len prepared to leave.

"Did jet lag finally catch up with you?" I asked her.

Len looked at me and shook his head. "No, she's been shining the stove, washing windows, and ironing that closet-full of wrinkled clothes.

I wagged a finger. "Mother, you're not here to clean."

"Well, I had to do something while Len was busy," she said. "You know me, can't sit still."

"She's got the place ready for inspection," Len said. "She even made my lunch."

I groaned. "I hope the place wasn't too disastrous. I hadn't planned on an early hospitalization. No telling what kind of mess I left behind."

Mom grinned. "It wasn't bad. Your new drapes haven't come, so I thought it would be a good idea to wash your windows."

I forgot I hadn't finished that chore. "Is the nursery ready?"

"It looks great. Len did a good job."

"That's a load off my mind, but Mom you don't need to DO anything."

"Don't you worry about me." She hugged me tightly before leaving.

At ten p.m., I fed Christie one last time before bedtime. The nurses decided I should sleep through the night so I would be rested for my big day.

*     *     *

A sleeping pill had afforded me a restful night, but my anxiety mounted as the morning wore on. When Mom and Len arrived, I pretended to be calm.

Soon, loaded on the gurney, I said good-bye, assuring Mom and Len I'd be back shortly. No ICU for me.

In the pre-anesthesia holding room, alone in the gloom, I fought to calm my quivering body and pounding heart by slow, deep breathing. The pre-op drugs that dried up every speck of spit caused my throat to feel constricted. I focused on breathing and tried to ignore the choking sensation. Just when I thought I would strangle to death, Miriam appeared. I recognized her behind her mask and instantly relaxed upon seeing my former coworker. Miriam told me she would be with me today, scrubbing once again.

Inside the operating suite, Dr. Green prepared me for the induction of anesthesia. I didn't see Dr. Larkin enter the room, but he must have been scrubbed and ready because Dr. Green said in his soft voice, "Debbie, I'm going to put you to sleep now."

*Thank God.* Then I dropped into a world void of dreams and sounds and worries.

243

*       *       *

"Debbie, wake up," a disembodied voice said. "It's all over. You're in the recovery room."

I climbed from the chasm of unconsciousness. A fire burned the back of my neck, and nerve endings throbbed, waking my sleeping brain. As if I had been inhaling vacuum cleaner dust, I coughed and squeezed down a painful swallow. I retched. My eyes tried to focus on my surroundings. Everything was a blur.

"We'll be taking you back to your room now," the voice said.

*Which room?*

*       *       *

# CHAPTER TWENTY-EIGHT—RECOVERY

Clink . . . jingle . . . clank. The familiar sound of some-one lowering a bed rail roused me. I opened my eyes and saw Len and Mom smiling at me. Behind them, baby gifts and flowers rested on a familiar table. I realized I wasn't in ICU.

"We're going to move you into your bed now," a female voice said.

Pain in my neck awakened when the recovery room nurses transferred me into bed. They propped, smoothed, and tucked me into a tolerable position, and then floated away as the anesthetic, coupled with the drugs, sucked me into an abyss and closed down my mind.

A minute or an hour later, I didn't know which, a sharp pain in my neck and upper back launched a moan from me. "Ohhh--" I dabbed a dry tongue over lips that felt like withered potato peels. Mom and Len loomed over me, poised to help. "Call the nurse," I rasped. "I need a pain shot. I need to move to a different position." I felt compressed, my head and neck cramped at an odd angle. But I was afraid to move, fearing the pain would intensify.

After the medication dulled a portion of my pain, the postpartum nurse attempted to turn me onto my side. She pushed, pulled, and twisted, battling my flaccid legs and sensitive operative site.

Stabs of pain lanced through my neck into my head, back, and arms. I thought my neck would separate from my body. "Stop! You don't know what you're doing! What time is it?"

"Four-thirty," the nurse said.

"Call Sharon. Beep her!" I barked orders like an ER doctor. "She's the 3-11 clinical instructor. Get her up here NOW. She'll show you how to turn a patient who's had back surgery." The nurse fled the room while Mom and Len stared at me.

Len frowned. "You didn't have to be so rough on her."

"She was hurting me."

"She meant well," Mom said.

Sharon, a hefty, fiery redhead, arrived quickly and demonstrated to the all the postpartum nurses on shift the proper method of turning and positioning a post-op back patient. She rolled my body as one unit, like a log, and positioned me on my left side, showing the staff where to place pillows for comfort and support.

"Thanks, Sharon. You saved my life."

"No sweat, kiddo. Call me if you need a repeat demo." She hustled away, and I promptly fell asleep.

A couple hours later, I awoke from my morphine-drugged nap, achy and exhausted, as if I had worked a week without a day off.

"Honey, dinner's here," Len cooed. He rattled a metal lid off a plate. "Mmm, we have pea soup."

The smell wafted my way, and I nearly gagged. I wrinkled my nose. "Not post-op pea soup. I hate pea soup." Instead, I sampled the gelatin and lapped water like a dog. The liquid fare assuaged my thirst and stemmed the fire in my throat. "What did the doctor find?"

Len moved the tray table aside. "Just what he thought—your birthmark wrapped like spaghetti around your spinal cord. He took a biopsy, and then he closed you up. That's about it."

I lifted my right hand to the bandage that covered my neck and upper back and was surprised by its size. "Well, he must've had a good, long look because it really hurts." Besides the IV in my left arm, I also had a urinary catheter, again. At least I didn't have to get up to pee. At least I wasn't in ICU.

Mom smiled at me, fingers tapping her chair arm. "I've been feeding Christie, and she's doing just fine on her new formula."

"Thanks, Mom. I'm glad you were here, but you should go home. I'll be fine." I wanted Mom and Len to stay, but they looked exhausted. Mom's makeup had faded hours ago, and Len's eyelids drooped. "You have a long drive. Get going. Don't worry. The night shift will be on soon, and my pals will take good care of Christie and me." I kissed them both, and they trudged out the door.

During the night, nurses monitored my vital signs, replaced IVs, administered medications, and repositioned me. In the morning, Dr. Larkin showed up wearing his usual grin. "Let's take a look." He tilted my head forward and whipped off my dressing, yanking out strands of hair caught in the tape.

"Ouch," I muttered.

"Looks fine." He reiterated what Len had told me about the surgery, and then he scribbled in my chart. "And we'll discontinue your catheter and the morphine but keep the IV for antibiotics. Tomorrow we'll get you out of bed and resume physical therapy."

"Great, we'll do that."

Dr. Larkin inspected my birthmark bumps and conducted the usual neuro exam. Nothing had changed. "If you need anything, just ask."

After he left, I rubbed my tape-burned neck. I couldn't imagine myself upright. I had to remind myself I had legs because they were still numb, and I couldn't will even one toe to move. My neck and back hurt so badly, I couldn't raise my head off the pillow. Nothing functioned properly except my arms, and an IV encumbered one of them. I ate my meals at a forty-five degree angle, slopping most of the food onto my chest. After the urinary catheter was removed, voiding was problematic, trying to find a comfortable position for my head and neck while perched on a bedpan.

Darvocet, the oral pain medication Dr. Larkin ordered, didn't ease my pain. Seeing my tears, the nurse called Dr.

Larkin and asked him to order something stronger. On the crest of Percocets, I survived my first post-op day.

The following day, per the doctor's orders, my nurse and physical therapist prepared to evict me from bed. Remembering past experiences, I requested a pain pill prior to the event. My helpers not only maneuvered my lifeless legs but also guided my head and upper body into a sitting position. My legs dangled from the bed as I struggled to maintain my balance and hold up my head, which seemed to weigh a hundred pounds. They eased me to a standing position, more or less, and hooked their arms under mine to support me. My legs wobbled but held me erect for a few moments. Then my knees buckled. They hoisted me and my rag-doll legs back into bed.

I guessed the doctor thought it best that I didn't lounge in bed and develop pneumonia or blood clots, or maybe he thought I should be strong enough to stand. But I wasn't. And the fresh operative site felt as if someone was screwing my head off my body.

I wanted to cry.

By Friday, my third post-op day, I felt more human and less like a wounded animal. Cathy, my physical therapist, coached me through the warm-up exercises designed to strengthen my muscles. Using a walker, I tried to take a couple steps, but depended on Cathy to keep me from falling. My legs didn't move where I wanted them to, as if they had minds of their own, and before I could make it to the door of the room, they crumpled as easily as paper.

I showed better coordination during my second and third therapy sessions that day. I felt my muscles responding to the grueling workout. One of the desired effects of the steroids was to impair the growth of blood vessels and reduce the size of my vascular malformation. I had to believe the steroids were helping.

During one of those exhausting bathroom visits, I caught sight of myself in the mirror. My reflection stunned me. My face was swollen; my hair hung in limp, oily strings; my head bowed forward like an old lady's. I peeked beneath my loose gown. My sore breasts sagged; my postpartum stomach protruded with indecency; needle tracks covered my arms; plus, I had begun to suffer from hot flashes. I was a wreck. When I saw photographs of myself from the recent baby shower, I cried. Would I ever look like the old Debbie?

I kept a smile on my face for Mom and Len by imagining I was home with my daughter and husband and everything was normal. For now, I had to be content to watch Christie doze in her bassinet next to my hospital bed. When she awoke and stirred with hunger, I couldn't go to her or comfort her or carry her. Nothing had turned out as I had planned. Maybe Dr. Larkin was right. Maybe I wouldn't walk again. I'd never be a proper mother to Christie, never work as a nurse, never appear normal.

Yet Christie's presence and her own fight inspired me to work harder. I knew my hormones were largely responsible for my feelings and would eventually stabilize. I refused to succumb to self-pity or depression. Lessons I had learned in my early years prepared me for this day, taught me to be tough. I would win this battle.

Then Dr. Kaufman arrived and told me Christie weighed six pounds and could be discharged. My little inspiration was going home.

"Can't she stay a few more days?" I whined.

"She's perfectly healthy and doesn't need to be here any longer," Dr. Kaufman said and then noticed my pout. "Tell you what, she can stay the weekend if you arrange care for her. But she can't remain in the nursery."

I smiled. "I can do that. My nurse friends and Mom and Len will pitch in to care for her."

Dr. Kaufman chuckled. "Okay, but Monday she must leave."

I nodded. "Before the hospital bigwigs return from their three-day holiday weekend and find an uninvited guest."

Over the weekend, Len, Mom, and Mary, my friend and former coworker, shared in Christie's care. Mom loved every minute she spent doting on her grandbaby. Although timid with Christie at first, Len fed and changed her, proving his competency and boosting his confidence. Mary accepted night duty, her (and my) usual shift. Although it was a holiday weekend, the usual hospital routine continued unabated—doctor visits, meals, drugs, P.T., baby care and feeding.

Before I knew it, it was Monday, the Fourth of July. Len and Mom arrived to take Christie home. Mom fussed over Christie while she dressed her in a pink sleeper and bonnet for the trip.

*I should be doing that. I should be leaving, too.*

I had no doubt Christie would do well at home with Mom and Len, but I'd miss her precious little face. I kissed her as she lay in the crook of my arm, savoring my last moments with her.

"We should get going." Len took the baby from me. "With this little pumpkin at home, you'll have an incentive to get better."

"I don't need an incentive. I'm sick of this place and can't wait to go home." I tried not to cry when Mom swaddled Christie in a light blanket and Len allowed me one more kiss. After they left, I surrendered to my sadness.

Since I no longer needed the services of the postpartum department, the nurses transferred me to another unit in the hospital—Six South, where I began my career at St. Joe's. Alone that night in my small, single-care room at the forgotten end of the hall, I watched Donny and Marie host a Fourth-of-July celebration on television. My eyes filled with tears, and the fireworks on the screen blurred into a collage of colors. I felt ugly, abandoned, and helpless. What had happened to my positive attitude? Isolated with my self-pity and tears of frustration, I prayed for strength to work harder toward recovery. The next day I would begin radiation treatments.

\*       \*       \*

## CHAPTER TWENTY-NINE—GET ME OUT OF HERE!

A transporter pushing a gurney barged through the doorway and interrupted my breakfast. "Time for your radiation treatment." He steered the gurney next to my bed. "Scoot on over."

I stuffed a piece of toast in my mouth. "I can't move my legs, and I just had back surgery."

"I'll need help," he grumbled and marched out.

"Typical," I thought as the boy left. I hoped the rest of the staff was more informed. The radiation treatments worried me. Would they help me walk again?

When I finally arrived in the radiation department, the transporter wheeled me into a dim, windowless room. He and another man dragged me like a sack of potatoes onto a narrow table, then hurried away for another pick up and delivery. I had just arranged my head in a comfortable position when a female technician breezed in and told me to turn on my stomach.

*Was she crazy?* I explained my situation—Cesarean section, sore breasts, back surgery, and paralysis.

Sighing, the tech tugged on the sheet and hauled me to the table edge so half of my body dangled in midair. Next, she rolled me onto my side and then reeled me back to the edge. With a jerk, she flipped me onto my abdomen. My body protested the prone position; sharp twinges knifed through my neck and upper back.

The tech strapped my head into a sling of sorts that immobilized me. While I waited for something to happen, I counted the blurry speckles in the floor tiles, feeling my cheeks balloon around the straps that held my face in a vise. My eyes watered, so I clamped them shut.

"I'm Dr. Rush," a man's voice announced. "We're going to do some measuring before the treatment. Should only take a few minutes."

"Okay," I managed to say.

The doctor and technician measured, plotted, and marked my upper back where the radiation would be delivered. Then they gave me my first tattoos to permanently define the radiation borders. I felt a pricking sensation when the doctor used a sharp instrument to deposit the inky blue dots. That didn't hurt, but every other part of me did. The pressure on my face irritated my sinuses, and I needed to blow my nose. Could I withstand this torture every day for six weeks?

At last, it was time to start the radiation. "Lie still. Don't move," the tech said. I heard footsteps scurry from the room, then a *thwump* as the door sealed me in my cave. Seconds later, a humming noise began, followed by clicking sounds.

*Here it comes.* I pictured a nuclear bomb blast, spewing radiation, and I tingled from the imagined fallout, saw my skin slough and my hair fall out. I sipped small breaths, terrified I'd move and misdirect the radiation, irradiate my lung or heart or spinal cord instead of the blood vessels of my vascular malformation. The humming and clicking sounds lasted a few minutes, and then I heard the door squeak open.

"You're finished," the tech said.

*That wasn't too bad.*

Over the next few days, I lathered up a sweat during my physical therapy sessions, pushing myself to take one more step. I expected the exercise to give me more energy, but the workouts and the radiation zapped my strength. I felt like an overworked hound dog that wanted to curl up and sleep. I noticed my legs getting stronger, but I had no control over them. Like a baby taking its first steps, I toddled through the halls stooped over my walker like a geriatric patient.

My walking wasn't the only thing moving slowly. A simple trip to the bathroom took effort and planning. I learned to allow for a thirty to forty-five-minute delay for someone to respond to my call.

One such time, when the nursing assistant finally entered my room, I told her I needed to put on my shoes to walk.

"Why do you need to put on your shoes?" she asked, hands on hips.

"They help my balance," I said.

"Well, that sure takes time." She jammed my Nikes on my feet and strangled the laces into bows. "Hurry up. I've got other patients and things to do."

"You'll have to help me sit up, and I'll need my walker."

The woman spun around. "Oh, for heaven's sake." She grabbed my walker and set it next to the bed with a clatter.

I held my tongue in my rush to get to the bathroom.

She assisted me onto the commode. "Put on your light when you're done." She firmly closed the bathroom door.

After completing my urgent business, I pushed the call light, but no one immediately responded. I decided to wash my hands while I waited. The stainless steel bathroom fixtures in the small enclosure reminded me of an airplane lavatory. The sink, operated by a foot pedal, hugged the wall to my left. I hefted my left leg forward and placed my foot on the pedal, but it wasn't strong enough to depress the pedal. Pushing down on my knee, I managed to produce a small trickle of water from the faucet. I rested my arms on my walker that was crammed in front of me, leaned toward the sink, and pumped soap into one hand. After an awkward wash, I realized I couldn't reach the paper towels, so I dried on toilet paper, remnants sticking to my damp hands. Still no sign of my helper.

For the better part of thirty minutes, the bathroom imprisoned me. I knew the call light was on, could hear its rhythmic buzz bleating in the hall. No one answered. I thought I could make it back to bed. The steel handles embedded in the walls on either side of me tempted me to pull myself off the toilet. It wouldn't be that hard. Yet a voice in my head warned against it. I knew patients suffered falls while in the hospital. I didn't need any more problems.

*How long does she think it takes someone to pee?* My head and neck hurt, and I was sure I had the imprint of the toilet stamped into my butt. My temper sizzled.

I grabbed the safety bars, gulped a couple breaths, and hoisted myself up. *I made it!* Quickly I seized my walker and steadied myself. Panting, I unlatched the handle, shoved my walker against the door, and flung it open. I sidestepped out, then hobbled toward the bed. Just as I was about to sit down, the nursing assistant returned.

"What do you think you're doing?" she asked.

"What do you think *you're* doing?" How dare she get uppity with me. She was the irresponsible one. "You ignore a bathroom call light for more than thirty minutes? Did it ever occur to you to check on your patient?"

"I was busy." The woman glared at me, then helped me into bed. Without a word, she removed my shoes and hastened toward the door.

Before she disappeared, I said, "Please have my nurse bring me a pain pill."

I waited, but no one came. I rang several times, begging for a pain pill, fighting back tears.

Finally, my nurse arrived an hour later. "Don't be putting on your call light for service every few minutes. I'm really busy." Kate, her name tag read, handed me the pill and a glass of water.

"I don't think going to the bathroom or asking for pain medication is demanding too much service." I swallowed the pill. "Send Rita in, and if she isn't here immediately, I'll be on the phone to Carla."

The nurse stalked out. I was so angry I wanted to cry. What had happened to this unit? Rita, the head nurse, used to keep her staff sharp. What had happened to nursing CARE? If Rita didn't show up, I'd call Carla, the division director.

Rita, my former head nurse, hurried in and made every effort to soothe me. Appalled by the behavior of her staff, she promised to remedy the problems. I knew she took the matter to heart because Carla, her boss, showed up to visit me that afternoon. We had a nice chat, but that didn't make me want to stay one minute longer than necessary. Although my coworkers and friends visited often, I missed Christie, Len, Mom, Bubbles, my bed, junk food, cable TV...

By Friday, my last day of radiation therapy for the week, I'd vowed to go home. When Dr. Larkin made his rounds and found me propped in a chair, I asked him to discharge me. "I've been here three weeks today, and I don't want to hang around here over the weekend. My next radiation treatment isn't until Monday. I can have Len and Mom help me with my P.T. at home."

Dr. Larkin studied me. "Let me see you walk."

I wriggled forward in the chair, grasped my walker, and pulled myself to a stand. I ambulated out the door and a short distance in the hall.

The doctor followed me. "Okay. You look pretty steady. We'll transfer your therapies to the outpatient departments." He reached for his prescription pad and scribbled orders, handing me the stack. "These are for your medications and for a walker to use at home. Dr. Ladisky, your admitting doctor, will finalize your discharge."

My smile felt wider than my face. "Of course. Thank you."

"I'll need to see you in the office, so call for an appointment." He shook my hand and left with a grin.

It took time to get discharged because all five of my doctors had to approve my discharge and issue orders. When Len arrived, I scrambled into the wheelchair as fast as my battered body allowed. I still couldn't sit in a normal upright position, so I settled into the car seat at my usual forty-five degree slant and sighed deeply. I was free. I was going home.

The thirty-minute drive intoxicated me. I drank in sights and sounds and renewed my relationship with the outside world. I breathed real air, despite a stage one smog alert, and achingly basked in the warmth of the sun streaming through the windows.

Soon Len exited the freeway and headed toward home. He drove into the garage, and Mom greeted us at the door with a smile. I wanted to jump out, but I had to wait for Len's help. He maneuvered me out of the car. Because my walker hadn't been delivered from the rental company, I clung to Len as I tottered into the house.

I stepped inside and didn't recognize the place. The freshly cleaned carpets, the thriving plants, and the spotless windows dazzled me.

I embraced Mom, fighting to maintain my balance. "Mom, the place is beautiful. You shouldn't have worked so hard."

"I didn't." She held on to me.

"I think you outdid yourself. Thanks, Mom."

"Come see the living room." She helped me move into the next room.

My new drapes, a weave of pale beige with a tinge of salmon, framed my spotless windows, in front of which stood a wicker rocker and green plants. The new furniture, a navy sofa with pale yellow flowers and a rust-colored recliner, looked inviting. I collapsed on the new sofa with a loud grunt. "This looks absolutely fabulous! Real homey."

"I think your choices were great." Mom took a seat in the wicker chair. "And how are you feeling?"

"Pooped," I said. "Where's my little angel?"

"She's asleep in the cradle," Mom said.

"What cradle?"

"Candy loaned you a cradle. I hope you don't mind that I put it in my room. I've been doing the night duty."

"That's fine." I was pleased my friend Candy had remembered. "Len," I shouted toward the kitchen, "you should be helping Mom at night with the baby."

Len hustled in the room and flopped on the floor, the dog right behind him. "I offered but she insisted."

"There's my Bubbles." I smacked my lips together to draw the attention of our eleven-year-old beagle mutt, but it preferred to lick Len's face. "How does the dog act around the baby?"

Len pushed Bubbles away from his face. "I think she's jealous."

"Me, too," Mom said. "She watches me hold the baby, wondering what's going on."

Bubbles wandered over to me, and I scratched her ears. "You're not top dog anymore, but I still love you."

Mom described for me Christie's routine and reported she was feeding well and seemed snug in her new surroundings. "One day Christie got a little fussy, so I put her in her carrier and set her in front of the stereo. When I turned on a country western station, she quieted immediately." Mom's eyes twinkled.

Len groaned.

"Are you hungry?" Mom asked me.

"I'm starved. I could eat a horse."

Mom rose from her chair. "Do you want to come to the table or the stable?"

I laughed. "I'll try the table." Sitting at the table hurt my neck, but I managed to make it through the meal before succumbing to a semi-reclining position on the sofa. "That sure tasted great. Nothing better than home cooking."

After lunch, Len had to return to work. "Call me if you need anything. You three girls have fun today."

He had just shut the door when Mom jumped up from her chair. "I hear a little fussing from the other room." Within minutes, Mom returned with Christie and placed her in my arms.

"Oh, I'm so glad to see you." I cooed to Christie. "How have you been? Did you miss your mommy?"

"I'll warm her bottle," Mom said.

"Have you been a good little girl for your grandma? I bet you had her jumping with each tiny whimper. You look bigger since I last saw you. Such a big, beautiful girl."

"Here you go." Mom handed me the bottle and pushed a pillow under my arm for support. She sat down in the rocker and smiled.

I couldn't stop smiling either.

\*     \*     \*

# CHAPTER THIRTY—REHAB ISN'T EASY

I never expected my recovery to be so difficult. I remembered how easily I had managed after my orthopedic surgery—visiting Jo the day after my hospital release, driving with Len the next day, and putting miles on my crutches. I realized I wasn't sixteen, but thirty-two hardly qualified me as geriatric. In my condition, ordinary tasks loomed as major obstacles.

A thirty-foot trek to the bathroom expended more energy than I had. My arms strained to support my weight, then quivered as gravity pushed me into the floor like a thumbtack. I forged ahead. With a frown, I bowed over my shiny new walker and demanded nerves to fire and move my lifeless legs. I wanted to quit, and I wanted to move forward.

Eventually, I arrived. I straightened up from my chicken-pecking pose and grinned at my reflection in the bathroom mirror. My smile vanished.

*You look awful.*

Tired hair curtained one eye. I flung aside the drape, and a bland face inspected mine, its color as washed out as old jeans. Overgrown eyebrows invaded a plump face where eyes shimmered, glazed from pain killers. I stretched lips into a pale line.

*You're a mess.*

Bathing involved forethought and planning. I couldn't stand for any length of time in the master bath shower stall nor rise from the tub in the guest bathroom. I didn't think to rent a shower seat, so I improvised with a towel-draped ice chest that barely fit in the shower stall.

Mom taped Handi-Wrap around my incision to keep it dry and helped me into the shower. "Are you sure you can manage?" she asked.

"I'll yell if I need something."

"Your walker is right here." She closed the door.

The tiny stall wasn't conducive to sit-down bathing. I stretched to reach the caddy holding the shampoo, soap, and conditioner, willing my arms longer and lighter. They felt as if they each weighed twenty pounds, but the warm water pouring over me soothed my strained muscles. Praying I wouldn't drop the soap, I washed away three weeks of hospital damage.

Twenty minutes later, enveloped in a wondrous steam, I heard Mom shout, "Do you need any help in there?"

"No, I'm fine. This feels heavenly."

Finally, I shut off the water and pushed open the door. My walker, serving as a towel rack, straddled the toilet. I inched forward on my perch, grabbed one leg of the walker, and hauled it closer. After drying, I pulled myself to a stand by sheer determination.

I yearned to blow-dry my hair and put on makeup, but after applying face cream and body lotion, I had just enough energy to wobble into the bedroom. After another twenty minutes of huffing and puffing, I managed to dress in something comfortable—a pair of maternity shorts and a top. Staggering behind the walker into the living room, I dangled a shoe stuffed with a sock by a free finger of each hand that gripped the walker.

Mom looked up from the tabloid in her lap. "You look refreshed."

I nodded toward my bare feet. "I can't put on my shoes."

"Let me help you." Mom slipped on my socks and shoes like I was a little girl. "By the way, your grandma and grandpa want to visit soon . . . if you don't think that would be too difficult."

I didn't know what to say. Grandma bossed everyone around, and I wondered how she and Mom would get along in the same house. I could already hear the German epithets. With Mom so busy, how would she handle two more people? "I don't really mind . . ." I let the words hang in the air while I decided what to say.

My mother sat back in her chair. "Mom can do all the cooking, and I'll do the cleaning and help with Christie. You know how I hate to cook, and your grandmother loves to be in the kitchen. She and Dad are so worried about you, and they can't wait to see the baby. You are their first grandchild, so you and Christie are special to them." Mom sounded as if she looked forward to her parents visit.

"If it's okay with you, it's okay with me," I said. "Besides we're going to need a lot of help around here. I have five more weeks of radiation and who knows how many more weeks of physical therapy. How do you feel about driving me to St. Joe's every day?"

"Gosh, I never thought about that." Mom grimaced. "Those freeways . . . so many lanes . . . so much traffic. They scare the heck out of me."

"You'll get used to them."

"What about Christie?" she asked.

"I guess we bring her along. Hopefully, I can get friends to take me a couple days each week so you can have a break from driving."

"That would work fine." Mom nodded and took a deep breath. "Are you ready now for your exercises?"

"I guess so."

Mom followed me into the bedroom. I slithered onto the bed, but without side rails or an overhead trapeze like I had on my hospital bed, I worked harder to turn or sit up. My arm muscles strained as I maneuvered toward the middle of the bed, and my elbows chaffed against the covers. I guided Mom through the exercise regimen designed by my therapist. When we finished, I lay unmoving, splayed like a dead butterfly on exhibit.

"Why don't you take a nap?" Mom suggested.

"Only if you promise to rest too while Christie's napping."

"I will." She leaned over and kissed me on the forehead.

I think I was asleep before she stood up.

During the weekend, I could almost believe at times we were a normal family. I had always imagined Mom coming to help after the birth of my child, but I never dreamed I would be so incapacitated or such a burden. Len pitched in with the shopping, cooking, and cleaning. Mom handled the washing and ironing, and she and Len shared in Christie's and my care.

I slouched on the sofa most of the day and wrote baby announcements and thank you notes. And I ate. The effects of the steroids made me ravenous. I chomped pretzels and chips as if my survival depended on devouring junk food. I avoided the scale, knowing I hadn't lost the weight gained during pregnancy. Medication relieved the pain in my back and neck, but I moved as if I were swimming through molasses. I only forced myself out of the muck to feed Christie and adhere to my exercise program. Although I loved being home with my family, I wished I could be more of a participant.

Len and I relieved Mom of night duty on Friday and Saturday. Every three hours Christie whimpered from her cradle at the foot of our bed, signaling her hunger. Len trudged off to warm her bottle while I wiggled into position to feed her. As long as I had Len to fetch things, I managed to feed and change the baby. Len and I snatched minutes of sleep, adapting to our role as parents, however unconventional the routine.

After the peaceful weekend and my adjustment to home life, my real challenge began Monday morning. Len helped me dress before he went to work while Mom prepared Christie for the trip to St. Joe's. After breakfast, she loaded the baby and her paraphernalia in the car and then assisted me. What an ordeal. I moved like a slug. Mom must have thought she'd never get me in the car.

Finally, Mom climbed behind the wheel, took a deep breath, and started the car. "Well, here we are. Just tell me where to go."

"You're going to do fine, Mom. I'll tell you which lane you need to be in. Don't forget to signal when you change lanes. And don't drive over any bumps." I laughed.

She threw the car in reverse and backed out of the garage. "Don't expect too much."

We arrived safely at St. Joe's, and Mom parked near the door of the radiation therapy department. Somehow she managed to get the baby and me inside without calling for reinforcements. I was quickly called for my treatment, which lasted about ten minutes. Dr. Braddock, the radiation specialist, explained he would periodically order blood tests, and the nutritionist would check my weight and dietary intake throughout the treatment phase. Inwardly I groaned.

The distance from the radiation department to the physical therapy department was farther than I could walk, so I hobbled back to the car. Mom packed Christie and me in the car again and drove to the P.T. department entrance. All the loading and unloading tested my stamina, not to mention Mom's. The wait for my P.T. was a bit longer, but Christie behaved like an angel. At last, the therapist called me to the exercise room—my personal torture chamber. Just getting there was work enough.

The therapist helped me lie down on a low, padded table and attached one-pound ankle weights to me. Like lifting cumbersome concrete blocks, I strained to keep my uncoordinated legs from teetering side to side. Lying on my back, then my side, and lastly my stomach, I repeated an identical sequence of exercises as sweat dampened my hair and puddled in my bra.

In addition to leg lifts, I performed wimpy sit-ups, pelvic thrusts, and knee squats. When I balanced my way through the parallel bars, my image in the surrounding mirrors startled me. Who was that chubby, awkward person? I averted my eyes and tackled the next set of exercises— tedious foot maneuvers designed to tune my fine motor coordination. Lastly, the stationary bicycle and treadmill tested my endurance, which at that point was nil.

I hated every second.

When my forty-five-minute session concluded, I head- ed to the waiting room like a whipped dog. Mom took one look at me, gathered up the baby, and hurried to get the car. Too tired to talk, I heaved a heavy sigh and collapsed onto the front seat, sore muscles quivering in fear of more punishment. I couldn't wait to do it all again the next day.

Back home, Mom put Christie down for a nap then made lunch. I absorbed as many calories as I could and tried to recuperate throughout the afternoon. Before the dinner hour, I struggled through my home exercises, showered, and prepared to greet Len when he arrived home. After dinner, Len did the chores so Mom could rest up for Christie's nighttime interruptions. I wondered how Mom and Len could sustain the pace.

The next day I called Dora, the nurse who worked as the nursing supervisor replacement for me and who lived nearby, and accepted her offer of help. She was more than willing to chauffeur me to the hospital one day a week. My friend Candy also volunteered for a day. I met Candy while attending one of Len's play rehearsals in 1980. Her husband, Hal, and Len had been rehearsing the comedy production "Murder at the Howard Johnson." Over the years, Len performed in several plays, usually in a dinner theater format. Although Len hadn't made it big in the "biz," he earned a few bucks pursuing his passion. Luckily, his present hiatus afforded him time for fatherhood.

\*     \*     \*

July days crept along, one like another. The radiation, physical therapy, and exercises became monotonous. The steroids wreaked havoc on my body, distorting my appearance into a pudgy-faced, lightly mustached, stooped, but still lame person. I hated to look in a mirror.

Apparently, my behavior had changed, too. One day as I slumped on the sofa and listlessly paged through a magazine, Mom asked, "Do you suppose you're depressed?"

I looked at her. "What?"

"Well, I was thinking maybe the drugs . . . maybe the baby blues . . ."

I tossed the magazine aside. "I don't have postpartum depression. And I'm trying to cut down on the pain pills."

"I just thought . . ."

"What? I should be doing more?"

"No, it's just . . ."

"Look at me. I don't even look like myself. I can't walk, can't carry my child, can't work, can't even take care of myself. Wouldn't you be depressed?"

"I know," she said.

But she didn't know. She didn't know how hard it was for me to sit on the sidelines while life, including my daughter's, marched past me. I tried not to feel sorry for myself, tried to remain positive, but I was disappointed not to see more improvement. Patience wasn't easy.

\*        \*        \*

# CHAPTER THIRTY-ONE—THE PLAN

To pull myself out of my supposed funk, I phoned my hairdresser and begged her for some help. Dawn agreed to make an emergency house call and repair my grown-out hairstyle. She added highlights, then cut and shaped my hair into a short, bouncy style I could easily maintain. Although still pudgy from the steroids, I stood a little straighter, with more pride and conviction, feeling more attractive than I had in a month. My new look improved my attitude and convinced Mom my "depression" was gone.

On August 1, Christie and I had our six-week checkups with our respective doctors. My baby butterball weighed nine pounds, a gain of three pounds since her discharge. I was surprised I had actually lost some weight. After the appointments, I worked out in physical therapy like a woman on a mission to lose her remaining pregnancy pounds and tone up.

The following week, I completed my radiation therapy treatments. Dr. Braddock explained that the effects from the radiation would continue although the treatments had ended, so I could expect further improvement. Sensations in my legs were returning, pinpricks feeling sharper where they had once been dull. I could almost feel the engorged blood vessels around my spinal cord shrinking to allow impulses to pass. The coordination in my legs and feet improved; my feet actually moved where I wanted them to go. Muscles also grew stronger, and the pain in my neck and back lessened. However, if I had any hope of returning to normal, I had to improve my balance and stamina.

"So, when are you going to get rid of that walker?" Len asked one day.

"I don't know. I still get tired and need to lean on it," I said.

"If you don't hurry your recovery, Christie will be walking before you," Len said with a laugh.

Although I knew he was teasing, I feared he was right. I had made great strides, but I was still frustrated by my slow progress.

My grandparents arrived days later for their two-week visit. Grandma seemed relieved to see me upright and breathing. She sniffled as she hugged me. I led my grandparents to Christie, who was dozing in her cradle, legs tucked under, butt in the air, oblivious to her audience.

"She looks just like Debbie when she was born," Grandma said.

"Such a little thing," Grandpa repeated over and over before he headed to the patio to smoke his pipe and play a game of solitaire.

After Grandma shared with Mom the latest hometown gossip, she assaulted the kitchen. Like a general preparing for battle, she took stock of the supplies and formulated menus. She baked and cooked endlessly from the day she arrived. Surprisingly, neither she nor Grandpa had ever been overweight, but I knew I'd have to be especially careful.

Mom and Grandma found an occasional free hour to shop and visit the local swap meet, leaving Grandpa behind to baby-sit. One afternoon, while Mom and Grandma were out, I heard Christie awaken with a cry.

Grandpa hurried into the living room where I was sitting. "The baby is crying. What should I do?"

I chuckled. "Bring her to me." He returned with Christie, carrying her as if she were the Thanksgiving turkey. "If you'll bring me a diaper, I'll change her." Grandpa grumbled and shuffled off again, returning with the diaper. "Thanks," I said. "Now I need you to heat up that pan of water on the stove and set a bottle in it to warm."

"Ach, Gott im Himmel. Where are those women staying so long?" Grandpa huffed.

I heard him rattling around in the kitchen and laughed quietly to myself.

Grandpa watched me feed Christie, the smile on his face holding up the wrinkles. He shook his head of wispy gray hair, and his shoulders quaked with a suppressed laugh. "Such a little thing."

When the women returned, Grandpa scolded them for their lengthy excursion and quickly retreated to the patio.

Grandma gathered up her great-grandbaby, sat in the rocker, and laid Christie on her knees. With a quiver in her voice, she sang, "Patty cake, patty cake . . ." Christie stared up at Grandma's face, eyes opened wide with fascination. Grandma folded together her bony fingers. "Here's the church. Here's the steeple. Open the door and see all the people."

Remembering the many times I had watched Grandma do her routine for the grandkids made my heart swell. I no longer had to worry how my grandparents would blend into my home.

With my radiation treatments concluded, I transferred my physical therapy to the hospital just blocks from my house. Mom dropped me off, drove back home, and returned when I had finished. The hot August days zapped my energy. The sun barbecued me on my long hike from the drop-off point to the therapy department and basted me a rosy tint. My clothes sopped up rivers of sweat and clung like plastic wrap. Then, my workout started. Afterwards I scraped together a smidgen of energy for the long walk back to the car.

To increase my endurance and build muscle, Len bought me a stationary bicycle and ankle weights. I used my equipment daily, did my best and then some.

One day, while we were chatting at the table after lunch, Mom revealed her "Help Debbie Plan." "I've been thinking about going home," she said. "Diane will be starting school, and I have to help her pack and go with Don to take her to Illinois State."

I knew the day would come when Mom had to leave. While I was happy my sister was starting college, I selfishly wondered how I'd care for Christie and myself, manage the chores, and get to therapy.

"Maybe Karla could help out," Grandma said. "She finished beauty school but hasn't found a job, yet. Been babysitting to get by."

My eighteen-year-old cousin Karla, the youngest child of Mom's brother, lived in rural central Illinois. "Do you think she'd be willing to come to California?" I asked.

"We won't know until we ask." Mom grabbed the phone.

After working out the particulars, Karla (and her parents) agreed, and she planned to arrive before Grandma and Grandpa left. To make certain I had extra help, my brother and his girlfriend planned a visit. Knowing reinforcements were on the way, Mom packed her bags.

Mom's departure saddened me as much as the day Christie left the hospital, but she forced me to face my motherly responsibilities. She knew I was ready for the assignment. I had my doubts.

Before she left for the airport, Mom hugged and kissed Christie. "I feel like I'm leaving my daughter behind," she cried. "I didn't mind waking up during the night to feed you. I've been your second mother."

Tears welled in my eyes. "I know she'll miss you, too. I wish you could stay longer."

"So do I," Mom said. "But now I have another daughter to help."

I hugged Mom, as if drawing one more speck of strength from her.

"Well, I guess we better be going," Mom said to Len, who was driving her to airport. She kissed Christie one last time. "I'm gonna miss my pumpkin." After a good-bye to Grandma and Grandpa, Mom gave a sluggish wave as the car pulled away.

Grandma took up the slack until Karla arrived a couple days later. After showing Karla her room, Grandma oriented her number five grandchild to her duties. During their overlapping stays, Karla familiarized herself with Christie's routine, the household appliances, and the car.

After another emotional parting with Grandma and Grandpa, quiet settled in the house. Karla took excellent care of the baby and safely chauffeured me to physical therapy. She did her best to stay on top of the laundry, cleaning, and dishes. Grandma had left us enough provisions for a month, so all in all, we were coping.

My brother, Roger, and his girlfriend, Cheryl, arrived in California near the end of August. They helped with Christie, did chores, and found a weekend to take Karla to the beach and Six Flags Magic Mountain. Soon after Karla had learned how to use the appliances and had gotten into a routine around the house, she suddenly developed abdominal pain and low-grade fever. I thought she had the flu, but when the pains became more severe one evening, I made Len take her to the emergency room. Tests confirmed Karla had gallstones. Doctors recommended surgery, but my aunt and uncle wanted Karla sent home for treatment. I agreed. She returned to Illinois after a week on the job, leaving Roger and Cheryl to help me for one more week before they had to go home.

With only seven days to regain my independence, I wondered what happened to Mom's great "Help Debbie Plan." What would I do without my family's help? If couldn't take care of myself, how could I care for Christie? I had never felt so challenged in all my life, but that only made me more determined to withstand whatever came my way.

I pushed myself through my exercise regimen that last week. In the house, I started using a cane. With the cane in one hand and Christie in my other arm, I wobbled through the rooms. Christie quickly adjusted to my strange locomotion, but I worried I'd stumble and drop her. I clamped a firm hold of her, thankful she was small enough to fit snugly in my free arm.

Before the month ended, Len's parents, Jo and Ken, moved to California. Amarillo hadn't suited them, and they decided to relocate in California. They were ecstatic to meet their new granddaughter, and their additional support was just the medicine I needed.

After Labor Day, Roger and Cheryl returned home, and Jo and Ken moved into their own apartment and started new jobs with a photography studio. For the first time in months, I was alone.

\*　　　\*　　　\*

# CHAPTER THIRTY-TWO—WALK ON

The silence in the house was a stranger. It made me uneasy, as if I were beginning second grade again and didn't quite know how to act. I missed the familiar smell of Mom's perfume and Grandma's talcum powder. I missed the sounds of voices—Grandpa's snatches of German, Mom cooing to the baby, Karla's lilting giggle, even my brother's speeches. Then Christie whimpered and reminded me I wasn't alone.

I tried not to let all my responsibilities overwhelm me, so I concentrated most on improving my walking and caring for my baby. Without a chauffer, I was forced to discontinue my hospital physical therapy. I substituted the baby stroller for my walker and pushed Christie to the park at the end of the paseo nearly every day, a quarter-mile trek. Sitting in a swing with Christie on my lap, I practiced fine-motor exercises with my feet. I continued my exercise program at home, and my strength returned as the pain dissolved in my determination.

In the middle of all the shuffling of my keepers, Len had changed jobs. Recruited by his old company and lured by a new sales manager, he quit his job at the Red Cross to return to the A.B. Dick Company, selling copy machines. To ensure that Len was up-to-date on the latest equipment and sales trends, the company planned to send him to Chicago for three weeks of training.

*What would I do without him?*

"Why don't you come with me?" Len suggested. "We'll fly to St. Louis, drop you off at your parents' house, and I'll go on to Chicago."

"Wow, that'd be great." I couldn't wait for Dad to meet his first grandchild.

Len and I worked out the details of the trip but didn't tell anyone we were coming, except my brother. When Len, Christie, and I surprised my parents, who were attending a barbecue at friends' clubhouse on the Kaskaskia River, I thought Mom would have a heart attack. She jumped up and down, hooted and hollered. Dad, pitching horseshoes nearby, heard the commotion, grinned, and sauntered over to welcome us. Three weeks later, I was back in California with Len and Christie, feeling stronger after the three additional weeks with Mom and Dad.

October was a time of adjustment and increasing my endurance. One load of laundry initially exhausted me. My upper back hurt from bending and lifting, and my legs just plain got tired. Some days I was so exhausted I felt like crying. But I performed my exercises and rode my stationary bike as if that was my job, so by the end of the month, I had increased my stamina to withstand mounds of laundry. I cooked easy meals, did some light cleaning, and tended to

Christie's needs. Len handled the grocery shopping and heavy cleaning while maintaining long work hours.

One evening, while Len and I were relaxing, I said, "I've been thinking about going back to work—part-time."

He turned toward me, a stunned look on his face. "Do you think you're ready?"

"I think I can manage four days every two weeks. One good thing about my job is the flexibility. I can have others help with the heavy lifting and patient transfers. My concern is holding up on the long walks between the nursing units."

"Well, I think you're doing a great job here at home."

I smiled. "Thanks. But my disability pay will run out at the end of the month, and we still have a stack of medical bills to pay."

Len ran a hand over his hair. "What about Christie?"

"As much as I hate the thought of leaving her, I think we need to find a sitter . . ."

Len shuddered.

". . . just one day a week," I said. "You can watch her when I work the weekend."

"Well, I guess that wouldn't be too bad. Do you think the doctor will approve of your plan?"

I shrugged. "I hope so."

"What about driving? You haven't tried that, yet."

I hadn't even thought about it. "You'll have to give me a test run."

Len laughed. "Okay. We'll go to the college parking lot, and you can practice. But if your legs don't perform properly—"

"Deal." I wanted to contribute to my family. And I missed my job. I knew I wasn't at my peak of health, but I felt ready for part-time work.

Dr. Larkin cleared me to return to work the early part of November. He believed I had almost reached my optimum level of recovery. I had finished the steroids a month ago, and my facial puffiness was subsiding. Since I had discontinued my physical therapy at the hospital, the doctor cautioned me to maintain my home exercise program to increase my strength.

Next, I had to find Christie a baby-sitter. Armed with a list of questions, I grilled prospective sitters. In the end, I chose to take Christie one day a week to the private home of a well-qualified lady. I prayed I had made the right choice.

I passed Len's driving test and convinced him I could operate the car. He agreed I wouldn't need a chauffeur to get to work.

When all the arrangements had been finalized and I was prepared to resume my career, a hint of apprehension nettled me. It crept into my mind like a piece of straw that works its way into your sock during a walk through a harvested cornfield. I tried to ignore it, but its chaffing demanded attention. What was bothering me?

I looked in the mirror and examined myself from every angle. I could stand to lose a few more pounds. But I had a decent hairstyle and my complexion was as flawless as Christie's. I wasn't beautiful or endowed with a magnificent figure, and, of course, there was my birthmark, still blooming in red and purple. Yet somehow I had managed to survive the taunts of my childhood and the difficulties of dating despite my difference. I was so used to seeing my birthmark that I didn't see it. I then understood why my parents had never talked about it—they never saw it either.

As I continued to study myself, I realized that my appearance hadn't hindered me. If anything, it made me who I was. My strengths weren't measured by how I looked but rather by my character and abilities. Perhaps that was why I was feeling apprehensive about returning to work. My performance wouldn't be up to my usual standard. I wondered if my coworkers would have patience with me as I honed my body to once again do my job. I wasn't totally recovered, but I'd do my best.

I slipped on my white uniform and laced my shoes, then threw my stethoscope into my bag and tiptoed into the nursery. Christie was stretched out on her side, breathing deeply. My eyes watered as I pulled the blanket over her and touched her cheek. I felt Len sneak up and place his arm around me, and we gazed at our daughter.

"She's going to be fine," he whispered.

"I know. I just hate to leave her."

Len hugged me. "Don't worry. Come on. I'll walk you to the car."

With sadness and a tinge of pride, I drove off.

I parked the car in the hospital parking lot, feeling as nervous as a new graduate nurse. The building loomed before me as I slowly ambled toward it. Four months ago I couldn't wait to leave the place, could barely sit up, and now I could walk—without a cane. A part of me wanted to use that cane to lean on, just to be safe, but inside I had walls for support. I could reach out and steady myself against their firm structure. They wouldn't allow me to fall.

When I stepped into the nursing office to reclaim my professional life, my coworkers smiled and embraced me, exclaiming, "You look great!"

"Okay, you're three nurses short," the evening supervisor warned. "Start calling your staff."

I smiled and released a breath. Nothing had changed.

*Everything was going to be fine.*

\*      \*      \*

*...for I have learned in whatsoever state I am,* therewith *to be content.*

*Philippians 4:11*

# EPILOG—DISCOVERY

During the decade following my daughter's birth, I once again took for granted my ability to walk. I was a busy wife, mother, and nurse, and the memories of my past paralysis receded from my thoughts like labor pains from a mother's. Then in 1994, the tide caught up with me when my legs weakened again. Their numbness and tingling sent me limping to Dr. Larkin. He ordered an MRI (magnetic resonance imaging) of my entire spinal cord and discovered spinal cord compression in my lower lumbar spine caused by my vascular malformation. Another six weeks of radiation improved the symptoms enough so I could hobble independently.

At my last visit with Dr. Larkin, I relaxed in a chair in his examination room while he perched on his rolling stool, studying my reports splayed on the tiny desk. I decided to ask, "Did you ever determine what's wrong with me?"

"Oh, didn't I tell you?" He grabbed a pad of paper and printed: Klippel-Trenaunay-Weber Syndrome.

I looked at the words. "That's what I have?"

He stumbled over the words. "Klippel-Trenaunay-Weber Syndrome or K-T, as best we can tell."

The name alone frightened me. I remembered Dr. Larkin telling me he had planned to write an article about my case for some medical journal. I had even posed for photographs in the hospital shortly after Christie's birth. "Did you ever write that article about my case?"

Dr. Larkin smiled and looked down at the bulging chart. "No."

Still stunned by the realization I had a foreign-sounding syndrome, I didn't care that he had failed to write his article. "So, what are the symptoms of this syndrome?"

"A port wine stain, soft tissue and bony hypertrophy, venous malformations, and lymphatic abnormalities."

As Dr. Larkin ticked off the symptoms, I could see how I fit the profile—my port wine stain, longer leg, and malformation around my spine. Other than the lymphatic problem, my symptoms were classic. I sat up straighter in the chair. "My goodness, that describes me. What else should I know?"

He adjusted his glasses. "It usually affects one limb. The bone and tissue often grow two or three times their normal size."

I patted my bigger left leg. "So that might account for my lopsidedness."

He nodded. "Yes, and the affected extremity is often the one with the port wine stain. The limb can also have lymph drainage problems and deep vein varicosities that cause it to swell. Occasionally the shorter, smaller extremity is the limb involved."

After all these years, throughout my entire life, not one doctor had diagnosed the cause of my symptoms or associated them with a syndrome. Why hadn't they figured it out? I shook my head and leaned forward in the chair. "I can't believe this. I finally know what's wrong with me." I grinned for a moment. "But my port wine stain involves my arm, not my leg."

Dr. Larkin smiled and rested his hands on his knees. "We don't know much about the syndrome; however, the port wine stain, a vascular malformation, does not regress, but it may change in color and texture."

I nodded. "That's why you had studied the bumps on my birthmark."

"Yes. I called it a hemangioma, but that's incorrect because a hemangioma grows rapidly from birth, then shrinks. You have a vascular malformation—one that grows as you do and never regresses."

"What about the blood vessels around the spinal cord?"

He frowned and took a deep breath. "I understand the malformation can affect internal organs . . ."

"Like my spinal cord," I said.

His smile reappeared. "Yes. Each case is different."

I slouched back against the chair and folded my hands in my lap. "I had no idea. What causes it?"

He shrugged. "No one really knows. It's congenital and might be the result of a genetic problem, but that hasn't been proven."

I heaved a sigh. "Is there any specific treatment?"

"Just control of symptoms." He glanced down at the reports.

"Will my problems with cord compression continue?" I clutched the chair arms like a vise.

Dr. Larkin looked up and swiveled toward me on his stool. "I don't think so. We didn't radiate far enough down the spinal cord the first time to eliminate the problem. Now with MRI, we can better understand what's going on inside you."

"I see. So the malformation is gone?" I held my breath.

"Yes. Still, I'd like for you to see Dr. Morton. He's on the Board of Rare Diseases and can provide you with additional information." Dr. Larkin turned back to the desk.

I released my breath. I knew Dr. Morton was a hematologist/oncologist, but I didn't know he treated rare diseases. "Okay, I'll see him if you think it will help."

After thanking Dr. Larkin, I hobbled from the office, clutching the slip of paper with the name of a syndrome I couldn't pronounce. Wait until Len heard this bit of news. Wait until I told my parents.

A few weeks later, I saw Dr. Morton and received a thorough physical and a few paragraphs of literature about

K-T. He suggested I might have to try a drug called interferon alpha, which inhibits cellular growth, if problems reoccurred. I didn't really understand the need for the drug if a vascular malformation didn't grow. The fact that my malformation had been irradiated didn't warrant the drug therapy. Unless I showed new signs of spinal cord compression, I wouldn't consider taking the drug.

At home, I studied the literature, shocked to learn that only 500 cases of K-T had been documented worldwide. I truly was a rarity. No wonder no one had made the diagnosis. When I was six years old, I realized I was different. At forty-three I finally learned why.

I booted up my new computer and, within minutes, I found the K-T Support Group website. I signed up to participate. I quickly discovered I was one of the oldest participants with K-T. Like me, some of the adults in the group had just learned they had the rare syndrome. The stories of their discoveries were as surprising as my own. Other participants were parents with recently diagnosed newborns, wanting information about the obscure syndrome.

For days, I stayed glued to the computer, followed the conversation online, and learned about the syndrome and the latest treatments. Laser therapy was now utilized to reduce the coloring of the port wine stain. Epiphyseodesis or epiphyseal arrest was now performed to assure equal leg lengths by fusion or metal fixation of the growth plate, meaning children no longer had to endure lopsidedness that resulted in scoliosis like I had experienced. When a child was diagnosed with K-T, doctors now performed MRIs and CAT scans to rule out internal vascular malformations that might pose problems.

What an age we lived in. Early diagnosis of K-T and appropriate intervention afforded affected individuals an opportunity to grow up normally. No child with K-T would have to suffer taunts and rejections because of a port wine stain.

I wondered what my life would have been like if doctors knew about K-T when I was born. It might have been easier, but I realized I was the person I was today because I grew up with that challenge of being different.

I called Mom and told her about my diagnosis. "We had you evaluated at Children's Hospital in St. Louis after you were born," she said a little too sharply.

"I know, Mom."

Mom's voice got louder. "We did what the doctors suggested."

"I know, Mom. They offered the best advice based on what they knew then. I read there were an estimated 500 to1500 cases of K-T world wide, but no one knows for sure. With so few cases, it's no wonder no one had heard of it. "

She softened her tone. "We treated you like a normal child."

I took a deep breath. "I know you did, Mom. You did fine. I'm not blaming you for anything. I think you and Dad handled my difference very well."

Mom's voice returned to normal. "Do they know what causes it?"

"No, they're not sure. You can read all about it online."

"I'll tell your father." Mom sighed. "Has anyone had their birthmark around the spinal cord like you did?"

"No one in the group that I know of. And many women with K-T have had normal pregnancies. But I learned some folks have their malformations around their bladder or lungs or kidneys. Everyone has their own unique challenges. I'm thankful my problems weren't worse than they were."

"How is your walking going?" Mom asked.

"Okay. Not as good as I had hoped, but I can get around. I started doing the exercises again, trying to strengthen my legs. I can't squat and stand back up, and my legs are still numb and tingly, especially after riding in a car. But I'm managing."

"Well, you take care," Mom said, as we ended our conversation.

Later that evening, while Len and I relaxed on the sofa, he asked, "So, what did your mom think of your news?"

"I think she was surprised."

Len smiled, wrapped his arm around me, and gave me a squeeze. "Well, at least we know what's wrong with you . . . among other things." He laughed, and I punched him on the arm. "I didn't know when I met you that you would go through life with crutches, canes, and walkers, but I love you anyway."

I hugged him. "I'm so glad you do. I love you, too." I snuggled into his arms.

THE END

CPSIA information can be obtained
at www.ICGtesting.com
Printed in the USA
LVOW04s1806280516

490396LV00001B/1/P